WAR: A SHORT HISTORY

War
A Short History

Jeremy Black

continuum

Continuum UK, The Tower Building, 11 York Road, London SE1 7NX
Continuum US, 80 Maiden Lane, Suite 704, New York, NY 10038

www.continuumbooks.com

First published 2009

British Library Cataloguing-in-Publication Data
A catalogue record for this book is available from the British Library.

ISBN 0 978 82642 276 7

Typeset by Pindar NZ, Auckland, New Zealand
Printed and bound by MPG Books Ltd, Cornwall, Great Britain

Contents

For Glenn Hall

Preface

The opportunity to write a short history of war is particularly welcome because of the importance of the topic if we are to understand past, present and future. The major themes of the book are all pertinent today: the variety of military environments, systems and methods of warmaking, and thus the need for caution in assessing capability. Rather than assuming, in any specific period, the global effectiveness of a particular army, the theme here is the extent to which a number of effective forces co-exist as they display best practice in specific contexts. The chronological divisions used in the book are designed to focus on 'world-scale' issues. In Chapter 3, the West does not have the dominant role it enjoys in Chapter 5, while in Chapter 6 the West faces greater problems projecting its power irrespective of its strength.

With space at a premium, it would be all too easy to present a clear account of readily apparent developments joined in an easy narrative. That would be to insult the reader. Clarity emerges, if at all, from an understanding of complexity, and war, its definition, causes, development and consequences, is highly complex. The Introduction introduces this theme, not least in the case of the definition of war, and complexity repeatedly emerges thereafter, underlining the extent to which discussion today about the nature of war has a long history.

Writing about war can seem to be overly distant from the grisly realities of combat and warfare. Such distance is not the intention here, and for much of human history there has been little attempt to hide the brutality involved. Indeed, the devastation was often celebrated. Weni of Abydos (*c.* 2375–2305 BCE), an Egyptian general who campaigned in Canaan (Israel) in *c.* 2350–2330 BCE, recorded in his triumph poem that his army had ravaged and flattened the 'Sand-dwellers' land': 'It had cut down its figs, its vines// It had thrown fire in all its dwellings// It had slain its troops by many ten-thousands'.

Horror, rather than celebration, was often evident. In 1791 CE a British participant in a victory over the powerful Indian ruler Tipu, Sultan of Mysore, noted: 'some of the poor fellows [Indians] had ghastly wounds . . . . Some wretches had half their faces cut off, some their hands lying by their sides; and two bodies I particularly marked which had their hands severed clean off by a single stroke, and lay at a distance from the trunks'.

I have profited from opportunities provided by lectures to develop my ideas. I am particularly grateful for opportunities to speak at the 2008 University of Virginia Summer School at Oxford, the 2006 and 2008 Rothenberg Seminars the Joint Warfighting Center of the US Joint Forces Command, the University of North Texas, High Point University, Union University, Adelphi University, the University of Texas, San Antonio, and Texas A and M University. I would like to thank Ian Beckett, Jan Glete, Wayne Lee, Jürgen Luh, Anthony Saunders, Patrick Speelman and David Stone for their comments on an earlier draft, Robin Baird-Smith for being a most supportive publisher and Sue Cope for her key role in the production process. None is responsible for any errors that remain. It is a great pleasure to dedicate this book to a good friend whose fine intellect matches his companionship.

NOTE ON DATING

CE (Common Era) and BCE (Before Common Era) are used. Those not familiar with these terms may read them as AD and BC.

Introduction

We were promised the end of war with the 'end of history' or with the obsolescence brought about by nuclear weapons. The reality has been very different. War has been a major aspect of politics since 1990, notably, but not only, in Africa, the Middle East and the Balkans. As I write, the Russians are invading Georgia while NATO forces are under pressure from a resurgent Taliban in Afghanistan. Furthermore, the threat of hostilities remains a key feature in world developments, not least, in terms of 'high spectrum' weaponry, with talk of future confrontation between China and the United States, and, at 'lower spec', with discussion of conflicts over resources, particularly water. On top of this comes terrorism, as well as conflicts within states. A key element of the modern world, and one that threatens to be an important feature of the future, war therefore deserves re-examination. This book sets out to do so by providing a short thematic history, with references forward to present and future.

Several points are worth underlining at the start. War is a key element in world history. Far from being Braudelian 'epiphenomena' of scant consequence compared to underlying realities, wars have played crucial roles in geopolitics, social developments, economic history and in the cultural/mass psychological dimensions of human life. War indeed is cause, means and consequence of change. Second, most work on war deals with conflict between states, but a key element, often the forgotten dimension, is that of the distribution and use of power within states and societies. Focusing on this provides a different narrative and analysis of military history and the history of war, and looks toward the present situation.

Third, Western interpretations of military capability and change are generally mechanistic, and deterministically so. These have a certain value, notably for sea and air capability, but are far less appropriate for land power and conflict. This situation is linked to the current crisis of Western military power, notably the contrast between output (force deployed and used) and outcome in terms of obtaining success. Fourth, non-Western traditions also have or had flaws, notably the cult of will (for example in imperial Japan), but they repay study in order to consider the past, present and future of warfare. Non-Western capability, moreover, is far more than a matter of the diffusion of Western weaponry and organization.

The key place of war in history emerges repeatedly in this book, which provides an up-to-date account of central themes and episodes. The major argument is for complexity – in what happened and why, and in the measure of military capability and development – and, rather than seeing this complexity and variety as a distraction from some sort of inherent core reality, they are presented as this very reality. Indeed, complexity and variety help to explain why military history is both important and fascinating. War also poses a puzzle. Bookshops groan with military titles, and, with biography, military history is the major historical topic in non-academic writing. Yet, there is not comparable academic attention and, indeed, some American military historians consider themselves an endangered species. This is paradoxical because conflict is a major theme in historical writing, while the relationships between war and state-building or war and society are major topics.

There are now a whole host of what could be seen as 'non-traditional conflicts' to which the term war is applied. These include war on drugs, war on crime, war on cancer, the battle of the sexes, generational conflict, culture wars and history wars; and that is not a complete list. Moreover, it can be expanded if other languages and cultures are considered. War, if not bellicosity, has therefore entered the language as part of an assessment of all relationships as focused on power, confrontation and force.

Warfare, however, needs to be abstracted from this language of war. Indeed, there is a need for a more precise definition in which war should be seen in functional terms as organized large-scale violence, and in cultural or ideological terms as the consequence of bellicosity. The first, at once, separates war from, say, the actions of an individual, however violent the means or consequences (one individual poisoning a water supply could kill more than died in the Anglo-Argentinean Falklands War of 1982); from non-violent action, however much it is an aspect of coercion; and from large-scale violence in which the organization is not that of war, for example football hooliganism. Each of these points and caveats can be detailed and qualified, but they also draw attention to fundamental issues of definition.

The cultural or ideological aspects of war also repay examination. They focus on the importance of arousing, channelling and legitimating violent urges, and of persuading people to fight, kill and run the risk of being killed, without which there is, and can be, no war. The willingness to kill is crucial to the causes of war and is a conflation of long-term anthropological and psychological characteristics with more specific societal and cultural situations. It is necessary to consider how far, and to what effect, these propensities to organized conflict have altered over time, an historical question, and one that emphasizes the point about bellicose drives varying by individual cultures.

The model of war as organized conflict between sovereign states, begun deliberately by a specific act of policy, is that which has been discussed most fully by theorists and historians. Thus, the grand title of Donald Kagan's interesting *On the Origins of War and the Preservation of Peace* (1995) reveals a study only of the Peloponnesian, Second Punic, First World and Second World Wars, and of the Cuban Missile Crisis of 1962. Kagan explains:

I am interested in the outbreak of wars between states in an international system, such as we find in the world today. The Greeks and the Romans of the republican era lived in that kind of a world, and so has the West since the time of the Renaissance [late fifteenth century]. Most other peoples have lived either in a world without states, or in great empires where the only armed conflicts were civil wars or attempts to defend the realm against bands of invaders.   (p. 10)

This overly restricted definition of wars worthy of consideration can be matched by the prominent British historian A. J. P. Taylor, who wrote of 'the more prosaic origin of war: the precise moment when a statesman sets his name to the declaration of it'.

Such an account of war might seem to have been made redundant by shifts through time, leading to the position today when non-sovereign actors such as insurgent movements and terrorist groups, most prominently al-Qaeda, play a major role, but, instructively, the clear-cut distinction between peace and war was even inappropriate for 1815–1945, the focus of Taylor's work and of much International Relations scholarship. It was inappropriate as an account, for example, for much of the warfare then arising from Western imperialism. More generally, any definition of war in terms of a public (governmental) monopoly of the use of force has to face both the contested nature of the public sphere and the role and resilience of 'private' warfare, both of which are major issues today.

Moreover, the rulers of sovereign states did not necessarily declare war on each other. In 1700, Augustus II of Saxony-Poland and Frederick IV of Denmark joined Peter the Great of Russia in attacking the Swedish empire, a war that lasted until 1721, but neither declared war. In 1726–7, the British blockaded the Spanish treasure fleet in Porto Bello and kept another fleet off Cadiz, dislocating the financial structure of the Spanish imperial system, while the Spaniards besieged British-held Gibraltar, but neither power declared war and the conflict did not spread. Indeed, the two powers became allies in 1729. Large-scale Chinese intervention in 1950 against the American-led United Nations forces in the Korean War (1950–3) did not lead to any declaration of war, and there were no hostile operations on Chinese soil.

The question of goals is raised when defining war in terms of intentionality (what were the combatants fighting for), but that approach also poses problems. In eighteenth-century India, military operations were sometimes related to revenue collections, often indeed dictated by the need to seize or protect revenue, but it is not easy to separate the operational aspects of wars that lead to a focus on gaining supplies from the widespread use of force to collect or seize revenue. The same point is relevant for many other societies.

The treatment of enemies as beasts or as subhuman poses other issues. Such treatment can be widely seen in conflict, especially civil warfare, as for example the religious wars of the sixteenth and seventeenth centuries in Western Europe. This treatment was also a feature in the genocidal drive of 'modern' states, most obviously Hitler's Germany. Indeed, the centrality of the Holocaust to Hitler's views and, finally, goals has been increasingly emphasized in recent years, and this has helped make the Holocaust a major part of our understanding of the Second World War. As such, the totally one-sided war on Jews becomes a conflict that should be considered as a war, and indeed Hitler regarded it as a meta-historical struggle. This is a point that can also be discussed in relation to other genocides.

More generally, if the savage practice of warfare – killing – can, for many, pose problems for any idea of war as inherently legal, because of the fact of sovereignty, or nobility, due to the test of battle, there is also the problem of whether and how far the practice of warfare can be legitimated by discussing it in terms of a benign goal. The use of saturation bombing and the atomic bombs in the Second World War are pertinent instances. Western intentionality was far more benign than that of the Axis powers (Germany, Japan, Italy), and the use of air power was effective, particularly against Japan in 1945, but, from the perspective of civilian victims, the situation looks less happy.

There is also the need to address the issue of the relationship between war and state development. The fifth-century CE Church-father St Augustine's comparison, in his *City of God*, of Alexander the Great of Macedonia, a key Classical reference point for heroism, with a company of thieves – 'in the absence of justice there is no difference between Alexander's empire and a band [*societas*] of thieves' – was a moralist's vain attempt to argue that intentionality, not scale, was the crucial issue, and that sovereignty was not a legitimator of slaughter. This point can be approached from a variety of directions, which can be grouped as ideological, legal and functional, without suggesting that this categorization is precise or uncontested. If a key issue with warfare is how it is possible to persuade people to kill, and to run a strong risk of being killed, then, for example, there was not much functional difference, in the sixteenth century, between 'state-directed' warfare and its *ghazi* (the Muslim system of perpetual raiding of the infidel) and, indeed, piratical counterparts. *Ghazi* raiding was often large-scale as with al-Mansur's campaigns in Spain in the tenth century against the Christian north, campaigns, focused on plunder and slave-raiding, which recruited *jihadis* and mercenaries from around the Muslim world. Spain was known as Dar Djihad, the land of *jihad*. Most spectacularly, the great pilgrimage destination of Santiago de Compostela was sacked in 997. The organized control, indeed killing, of humans was central to these different types of warfare, even if the objectives behind this control and killing were different. 'States' were inchoate, and not generally seen as enjoying the right to monopolize warfare and alone to initiate and legitimate conflict.

Today, issues of legitimacy come into play, not least with the claim to the attributes of sovereignty, including waging war, by groups not recognized as such, for example al-Qaeda, but also with the rejection of the idea that sovereign governments have a monopoly of force, and with moves toward supra-national jurisdiction through the United Nations and international courts. This question of the acceptability of conflict overlaps with the issue of the distinction between military and civilian as combatants, one that is at the heart of the legitimization of the modern Western practice of force and the legalization of Western high-technology warfare.

Furthermore, the use of force by (major) states against those they deem internal opponents or international reprobates cannot be rigidly separated from definitions and discussion of war simply because the states do not accept the legitimacy of their opponents. Turning to the past, there was a distinction between wars begun by imperial powers, such as Ottoman Turkey, Safavid Persia, Mughal India and Ming or, later, Manchu China, with outside polities, and, on the other hand, conflict within these empires, but the latter, indeed, could be large-scale, more so than external warfare, and could be regarded by contemporaries as war. Moreover, since each of these states rested on warfulness, war and conquest, they had highly bellicose values. When I asked the Mughal specialist John Richards to explain the propensity of the Mughal rulers for war, he used the analogy of a bicyclist to describe the Mughal empire and war: if it was not fighting, it would collapse. Through fighting, however, it did in the end do so.

It is difficult to determine whether attempts to overthrow these or other states, or to deny their authority, many of which took the form of rebellions, should be regarded as functionally sufficient and intellectually different to conflicts between sovereign powers not to be classed as wars. This raises the question whether it is only outcome that earns the designation war, an aspect of history belonging to the victor. Empirically, this is a question posed by the contrast between the American War of Independence (1775–83) and the unsuccessful Irish rebellion/revolution of 1798 against British rule, and also by disagreements over whether the unsuccessful Indian Mutiny (1857–9) should be referred to as a mutiny, a rebellion or a war of independence against Britain. This question feeds directly into modern revolutionary claims about struggles as wars.

More generally, the absence of strong, or even any, police forces frequently ensured that troops were used to maintain order and control, as is also the case in many countries today. That, again, raises the question of a definition of war as the use of force, in other words through function rather than intention. Given the role of the military in many countries, for example much of Latin America, as the arm of the state, with its prime opponents being internal, this approach directs attention to civil violence, if not civil war, and the para-military policing involved, as a prime instance of war. Any working definition of war has to be pertinent for Paraguay as much as the United States, and not least because a diffusionist model of military definitions and practice (i.e. modern American definitions and practice are adopted elsewhere) is nowhere near as applicable as some might imagine.

Turning to culture, the use of the concept of bellicosity (warfulness) not only counteracts the idea that the causes of war involved rational actors and rational calculations but also, in part, overcomes the unhelpful distinction between rationality and irrationality in leading to war. Bellicosity can be regarded as both, or either, a rational and an irrational response to circumstances. To refer to bellicosity as a necessary condition for, and, even, definition of war, is not to confuse cause and effect, or to run together hostility and conflict, but to assert that, in many circumstances, the two are coterminous. Bellicosity also helps explain the continuation of wars once begun. An emphasis on bellicosity leads to a stress on the assumptions of ruling groups, assumptions that are often inherent to their existence and role.

Such an emphasis also underlines the extent to which both sides have to be ready to fight, and to continue fighting, if war is to start and last. An emphasis on will emerged clearly from the account by the Greek historian Herodotus (*c.* 485–425 BCE) about the response to the Persian invasions of Greece in 490 and 480 BCE. In the first case, he reported Miltiades the Younger outlining what was at stake for Athens, one of the leading Greek city-states:

> if we forbear to fight, it is likely that some great schism will rend and shake the courage of our people till they make friends of the Medes [Persians]; but if we join battle before some at Athens be infected by corruption, then let heaven but deal fairly with us, and we may well win in this fight.

Miltiades' tactics were to bring victory at Marathon in 490 BCE, with the invading Persian army charged down by rapidly advancing Athenian hoplites or heavy infantry carrying long spears and large shields, who broke the wings of the Persian force before turning in on the stronger Persian centre. Herodotus also noted a widespread reluctance in Greece to fight in 480 BCE:

> the great part of them had no stomach for grappling with the war, but were making haste to side with the Persian. . . . Had the Athenians been panic-struck by the threatened peril and left their own country, or had they not indeed left it but remained and surrendered themselves to Xerxes, none would have essayed to withstand the king by sea. . . . I cannot perceive what advantage could accrue from the walls built across the Isthmus [of Corinth] while the king [Xerxes] was master of the sea . . . by choosing that Hellas [Greece] should remain free, they [the Athenians] and none others roused all the rest of the Greeks who had not gone over to the Persians, and did under heaven beat the king off.

The 'wooden walls' of the Athenian fleet were to save Greece at the Battle of Salamis. In the face of the larger Persian fleet (about 800 ships to the Greek 300), the Greeks decided to fight the Persians in the narrows of Salamis, rather than in the open water, as they correctly anticipated that this would lessen the Persians' numerical advantage. The Persians indeed found their ships too tightly packed, and their formation and momentum were further disrupted by a strong swell. The Greeks attacked when the Persians were clearly in difficulties, and their formation was thrown into confusion. Some ships turned back while others persisted, and this led to further chaos which the Greeks exploited. The Persians finally retreated, having lost over 200 ships to their opponent's 40, and with the Greeks still in command of their position.

In recent decades, there has been a growing reluctance to fight in many societies, certainly in comparison to the first half of the twentieth century, although the popularity of war toys, games and films suggests that military values are still seen as valuable, indeed exemplary, by many, or at least as an aspect of masculinity. Partly thanks to growing professionalism and the abandonment of conscription in many Western states, the military there is less integrated into society, both into social structures and into concepts of society. This demilitarization of civil society leads to a decline in bellicist values: instead, they are expressed through sporting rivalries or as a response to media portrayals of violence. There has also been a 'civilization', 'civilianization' or process of civilizing of the military. It can no longer be an adjunct of society able to follow its own set of rules, but is expected to conform to societal standards of behaviour, for example, in the treatment of homosexuality.

Yet, as recent years have shown, these changes do not have to mean passivity and the absence of war. Indeed, a range of issues, including pressures and tensions latent in globalization, and the response, can readily lead to the use of force. Moreover, whatever the current of social change, democracies, once roused, can be very tenacious in war, or at least their governments can be.

The suggestion that the 'West' has become less bellicist might also seem ironic given its nuclear preponderance, the capacity of its weapons of mass destruction and the role of its industries in supplying weaponry to the rest of the world. Indeed, it might almost be argued that this strength is a condition for the decline of militarism. A decline in bellicosity, in so far as it has occurred, could also be seen as owing something to the prevalence and vitality of other forms of 'aggression', for example, economic and cultural imperialism as a substitute for war.

An emphasis on the cultural contexts within which war is condemned by many but also understood, even welcomed, by others as an instrument of policy, and as a means and product of social, ethnic or political cohesion, is, also, in part, a reminder of the role of choice. As such, this approach is a qualification of the apparent determinism of some systemic models. A denial of determinism also opens up the possibility of suggesting that the multiple and contested interpretations of war by contemporaries, both today and in the past, are valuable, which underlines the importance of integrating these interpretations into explanatory models.

As far as intentionality is concerned, bellicosity leads to war, not so much through misunderstandings that produce inaccurate calculations of interest and response, the war by accident approach, but, rather, from an acceptance of different interests, and a conviction that they can be best resolved through the use of force. As such, war can be the resort of both satisfied and unsatisfied powers. The resort for war is also a choice for unpredictability, which is not simply the uncertain nature of battle, but an inherent characteristic of the very nature of war. The acceptance that risk is involved in warfare, and the willingness to confront it, are both culturally conditioned, not to mention the cultural role of rage leading to war.

This book seeks to show not only that military history is important, but also that a short military history of the world does not have to dispense with scholarly topics and debate. Instead, there is an introduction to key issues, notably the value of the idea of military revolutions, the extent to which it is valid to write of a Western way of war and the question of where the emphasis should be placed in the coverage of military history. These issues are introduced not only because they are significant but also because they serve to underline the extent to which the subject is an active one, with important controversies that are of direct relevance for the world today.

1

Until the 'Barbarian' Invasions

From the outset, in their search for food and shelter, humans competed with other animals. Fighting, indeed, is integral to human society; fighting is not, as often suggested, a result of the corruption of primitive virtue by the selfishness of developed societies. There was less contrast between such struggles with animals and fighting other humans than in modern culture. Moreover, the pattern of doing both, and celebrating both in ritual and culture, in longstanding modern hunter-gatherer societies, such as those in Amazonia and New Guinea, indicates a situation that was formerly far more common.

When our biological ancestors first roamed the plains and forests of the world, they, without weapons other than their hands and teeth, were intensely vulnerable to some other animals. Moreover, they also needed to kill these animals in order to obtain food. Weapons were crucial, both to fight off predators, such as bears and wolves, who attacked them, and also to become more successful predators themselves. Early weapons were based on stone that had been worked with other stones in order to make it more effective: chipped in order to create killing points. Spears and arrows were originally sharpened wood and later stone-tipped. As a result of the use of weapons and of organization in groups, around the globe, hunter-gatherers became more successful and more dominant in the animal world in the prehistoric period.

The dates of developments in weaponry are necessarily imprecise and their order is often unclear, but these developments stemmed from the growth of a tool-based culture. In about 100,000 BCE, stone tools, shaped by striking flakes from the core, started to be made. Humans were able to make successful weapons, especially composite tools – points and blades mounted in wood or bone hafts – which were developed in areas of early settlement, such as Israel, about 45,000 BCE. Bows and arrows, harpoons and spear throwers were used in Europe from about 35,000 BCE, and there are early Spanish cave paintings (from 10,000 to 6000 BCE) that depict organized men fighting each other with bows and arrows. Clovis points, made by chipping rocks into sharp flat shapes in order to produce large stone points able to pierce the hides of mammoths, were used from about 10,000 BCE in North America.

Weapons alone were not the key to human success. They also had important physiological and social advantages over other animals. Humans could perspire and move at the same time, a major benefit in both pursuit and fighting. Other animals, in contrast, stopped to perspire, and were therefore more vulnerable to attack. The human capacity to communicate through language was also very valuable as this capacity was linked to the ability to organize into groups, a vital skill when hunting herds of huge animals such as mastodons and mammoths, although lions and wild dogs shared this ability. The human use of language became increasingly complex.

Humans were also able to develop their tools, which was to become a key characteristic in the history of war and an aspect of the action-reaction and problem-response processes that were so important to human development. Humans tested the opportunities of everything they could lay their hands on – stone, wood, bone, hide, antler, fire and clay – both on their own and in combination. About 10,000 BCE, for example, the Japanese began to use bows and arrows, which gave greater penetrative power than the spears and axes previously thrown at other animals. Humans were increasingly able to confront other carnivores, which reduced the competition they posed for food, as well as their threat to humans. The human population grew because of the better climate after the Ice Age, and also their development of agriculture, which together helped the potential of humans to succeed. Bears, wolves and other competing carnivores were gradually driven away from areas of human settlement and into mountain and forest fastnesses.

The focus of human conflict, instead, swung to organized conflict between humans, which may, at some level, have been the case from the outset of human society, or at least from when foraging clans came into contact with each other. The oft-made argument that early warfare was ritualistic and partly, as a result, limited has to be handled with caution as evidence for the purpose and nature of early warfare is limited.

Weaponry certainly continued to improve. In 7000–5000 BCE, in both West Asia and South-East Europe, it was discovered that heating could be used to isolate metals from ore-bearing deposits. Soft metals, which melt at low temperatures, were the first to be used, and this explains why copper was the basis of metal technology before iron. The Stone Age began to be replaced by the successive ages of metal, but the concept of a revolutionary change in this process is problematic. Instead, there was a considerable overlap of flint tools (including weapons) with copper, copper with bronze and bronze with iron, rather than a sudden and complete supplanting of one technology by another. Otzi, the iceman from roughly 3000 BCE, had a copper axe, a flint knife and flint-tipped arrows with bow, and he was wounded, if not killed, by similar weapons.

In addition, the metallurgical aspects of making and processing the metals and alloys were not static, and different processes developed in particular parts of the world. In the third millennium BCE, bronze, which was made by alloying copper with tin, was widely adopted, as it was stronger and more durable as a weapon than pure copper. Metals offered greater potency than stone, not least because they provided stronger penetration and weight, the key requirements for success in hand-to-hand conflict, with the additional factor of the reduced bulk necessary for ease of use and mobility. This limited bulk was made more important by the extent to which nomads in this period usually migrated and fought on foot, rather than on horses or camels. Metal weapons generally favoured more complex societies once metalworks required the gathering of different resources and of labour. Bronze demanded copper and usually long-distance trade for tin, as well as smelting. This was a more complex operation than using flints.

Skill was involved in the development of weaponry, for example the composite bow, evidence of which dates from Mesopotamia (modern Iraq) in about 2200 BCE. Storing compressive and tensile energy by virtue of its construction and shape, allowing it to be smaller than the long bow, the composite bow was a sophisticated piece of engineering that seems, like some other early weapons, to have been invented in different places by various peoples, although there was probably some interchange of ideas. The composite bow, which was developed in regions where wood suitable for longbows was absent, was more effective than the simple bow, because its stave of wood was laminated, but its manufacture was labour-intensive.

Social change helped alter the nature of war. This change was linked to economic transformation with the move from hunter-gatherer societies to those focusing on specialized agriculture, both pastoral (animals) and arable (crops). These agricultural practices certainly supported a higher population density than hunter-gatherer societies. Moreover, the spread of agriculture accentuated the development of permanent settlements.

Economic development was linked to social differentiation, not least the emergence of élites providing political direction. This shift took a bellicose form, particularly with the combination of warrior deities and their royal representatives, and also as these élites fulfilled goals (including both expansion and security) and sought fulfilment through engaging in conflict. The militarization of societies became more apparent. For example the Bronze Age site of Motilla del Azuer in central Spain has numerous fortified mounds constructed between 4,200 and 3,500 years ago. The later Iron Age Celts built hill forts (*castros*) in Spain, such as the one at Castro de Rei, and metal smelting was common there. On the island of Sardinia, *nuraghe* (circular stone towers) were built for protection against pirates.

More generally, the scale of fortifications, for example of the high thick stone walls of Anatolian cities in the Early Bronze Age, such as Troy, indicates the extent of anxiety and threat in this period. Similarly, wars for domination within Early Dynastic Egypt (3150–2687 BCE) led to massive mud-brick walls for cities. The construction of a new mud-brick walled capital at Memphis, the White Fortress, in about 3040 BCE was a key act in the unification of Egypt.

Developments were not only defensive. Horses were domesticated as early as 4000 BCE north of the Black Sea, and by 1700 BCE were being used in a new weapons system, the war chariot, which proved important not only militarily but also as a way both to differentiate between soldiers and to organize the battlespace. Chariots eventually used spoked rather than solid wheels, which reduced their weight, and reins linked to bits provided a means to control the horses. Chariots served as platforms for archers.

The resulting armies were dominated by an élite of chariot warriors, to which the peasant infantry were distinctly secondary. The chariot kingdoms made a major impact in the Middle East, with the Hittites, whose Anatolian kingdom was based on a fortified citadel at Hattushash, which was particularly important. The Hittites sacked Babylon (in Mesopotamia) in 1595 BCE and contested control of Syria with Egypt, not least with the indecisive Battle of Kadesh in about 1274 BCE, a major chariot clash. The bas-relief monument at Thebes in Egypt depicts Rameses II of Egypt at Kadesh as a chariot rider, indicating the prestige of the role.

Weapons were significant, but to be most effective they needed to be wielded by large numbers of trained men, which required the development of states capable of the degree of control necessary to secure an agricultural surplus able to support permanent military forces organized by a central administration. These forces were different from those of tribal warfare societies, with a far greater level of mili-tary sophistication, although the states shared the sense that wars were waged at the behest of gods concerned to restore cosmic order and acting through divinely ordained kings. A series of empires based on conquest developed, especially centred in areas where agriculture was most able to support a high level of population. The environmental needs of growing crops meant that such empires existed only in certain parts of the world, especially China, India, the Middle East and the Mediterranean basin, and later in Mesoamerica.

Some empires displayed considerable military sophistication, for example the Assyrian Empire (based in modern northern Iraq) of 750–600 BCE in which disciplined formations of heavy infantry (armoured spearmen) co-operated on the battlefield with cavalry. The Assyrian state was one of the first to incorporate cavalry. The Assyrians moreover used heavy chariots, with four rather than two horses, and carrying four rather than two men, which increased their firepower. The Assyrians also had impressive siege capabilities, including mobile siege towers and covered battering rams. They conquered not only Mesopotamia, taking Babylon in 689 BCE, but also, in 663–671 BCE, Egypt. Just as the Hittites regarded themselves as benefiting in war from the support of the Sun God and as serving the purposes of the gods in their campaigning, so the Assyrians saw themselves as spreading the domain and worship of their god Ashur. However, the ferocious style of Assyrian rule, which involved mass killings, torture and deportation, failed because it bred hatred that fostered rebellions.

Siege engines were a product not only of technological sophistication, but also of resources and organization. Their development reflected the action–reaction cycle that is so important in military history. For example, by the late-fourth century BCE, in response to important developments in the scale of fortifications, the siege towers of the Hellenistic powers that contested the legacy of Alexander the Great become larger and heavier, able to project more power, and also were better defended, for example with iron plates and goatskins to resist the fire missiles and catapult stones launched from the positions they were attacking. The towers were assemblable so that they could be taken on operations. Moreover, the effectiveness of battering rams was enhanced by sheathing them with iron and mounting them on rollers.

In turn, the continued viability of nomadic pastoral societies ensured a contrast with those based on cultivation, a contrast that provided a context for competition as well as co-operation. The threat posed by nomadic or less settled peoples was particularly acute, as they were able to operate very effectively and were less ready to respect borders. For example, Cyrus the Great of Persia, who had considerable success in conquering settled states, defeating Croesus, King of Lydia (west Turkey) in 547 BCE and capturing Babylon in 537 BCE; creating a far-flung Middle-Eastern empire in the process, was killed by the nomadic Massagetae when he campaigned in Central Asia in 530 BCE.

With space at a premium, the emphasis here is on China rather than on the states in the Middle East and Mediterranean that have been seen as the background to Europe's development. This emphasis is a response to the importance and continuity of China's history as well as the value of approaching world military history through the Chinese perspective. As with the Romans, however, the problem is that we know most Chinese military history in and through the context of state power, chiefly because the records of such activity survives best, certainly in comparison with nomadic leaders. The Roman ability to create and maintain records was such that we also know a reasonable amount, albeit from the Roman viewpoint, about their opponents, such as the Carthaginian general Hannibal, and also Julius Caesar's unsuccessful opponent in Gaul, Vercingetorix. Each was defeated, Hannibal in the Second Punic War (218–202 BCE), and, as so often prior to modern times, we know most about the defeated from the victors' perspective.

In China, the urban civilization of the Shang dynasty developed in about 1800 BCE in the valley of the Yellow River, although this civilization was only a fraction of the size of modern China, and control beyond the core Shang territory was limited. The use of chariots, composite bows and bronze-tipped spears and halberds developed in the second millennium BCE. Conflict played a major role in the history of China. There was pressure both from regional tensions and from border people. The Zhou dynasty (c. 1050–256 BCE), originally a frontier power to the west that had overthrew the Shang, was, in turn, attacked by border people, especially the Di and the Xianyun from the bend in the Yellow River to the northwest.

There was a marked change in the character of Chinese warfare during the Warring States period (403–221 BCE), in which warring regional lords ignored and finally overthrew the weak power of the Zhou. These lords became in effect independent. The most successful of these dynasties in the end was the Qin, who, in 221–206 BCE, ruled all of China after a major series of conquests by King Zheng (r. 247–210 BCE). Zheng took a new title, First Emperor, for himself. The scale of conflict grew, a development that drew on organizational strength, and led, in the fourth and third centuries, to the development of military treatises, for example those of Sunzi [Sun Tzu] and Sun Bin. This attempt to provide a rational account of conflict and how to ensure success was important for the establishment of a self-referential analysis of warfare, one that encoded lessons of interest to later generations.

There were important qualitative changes in Chinese warfare. With iron metallurgy, the understanding of which was imported from Central Asia, the scale of weapons production increased, and, with more iron weapons, infantry became more effective. The rise of mass armies, a product of Chinese population growth and the introduction of conscription, ensured that chariots no longer played an important role. Much of the Chinese infantry was armed with spears. As another reminder of the importance of diffusion, cavalry was introduced from the fourth century BCE, as the northern Chinese state of Jin responded to the horsemen of non-Chinese peoples to the north. This response was a matter not only of access to horses from the steppe but also to cavalry techniques. Moreover, siege warfare developed with the use of siege towers and stone-throwing catapults against the thick earth walls built around Chinese cities.

The organizational sophistication of China was shown in the ability to construct a series of walls, including the Long Walls of Wei, Zhao and Yan (*c.* 353–290 BCE), which also testified to the sense of challenge from the nomadic people in the arid steppe north of China and their well-trained mounted archers. This challenge continued to be the case. Zheng's death in 210 BCE was followed by conflict in the ruling family and rebellion, with the eventual civil war won by Gaozu, who took the title King of Han. The Han dynasty (206 BCE–220 CE) built a new Great Wall to provide protection against attack from the north and also established a system of garrisons to give cohesion to its expanding empire.

There was a clear parallel with the Roman Empire, which was created in the same period. For both China and Rome, the combination of a growing population and the extension of control ensured greater resources to use for war and other purposes, for production and power were closely linked to population. Conversely, large armies were a challenge to the prosperity of an empire, both absorbing resources and lessening the ability to produce new ones other than through conflict. Thus, maybe up to a quarter of a million Italians were in the Roman army in 31 BCE, nearly a quarter of the men of military age. This level was unsustainable, as well as dangerous, encouraging Augustus (see pp. 25–6) to cut the number of troops in the legions to close to 150,000 men.

Like the Romans, most obviously with the crushing defeat by German tribes of three legions in the Teutoburg Forest (archaeologists now favour Kalkriese near Osnabrück as the battleground) in 9 CE, the Han also encountered limits. These limits indicated the extent to which, like later military systems, there were constraints within which even the most successful empires operated. Indeed successful military organizational structures in part tended simply to mean that the borders of empire were more far-flung. The borders could then be fixed with military colonies and walls, such as the rampart and palisade constructed by the Romans between the Rivers Rhine and Danube, as well as Hadrian's Wall in northern England, which was at once a means to regulate the frontier and to defend it if necessary.

The Han were challenged by the formidable Xiongnu confederation of nomadic tribes, which was unified in 210–209 BCE, and was the first empire to control all of Mongolia. The Han responded to the Xiongnu not only with walls but also with large-scale offensives during the years 201–200 BCE, a disastrous policy that ended with the army encircled and the Emperor suing for peace. These offensives were resumed in 129–287 BCE. To indicate the scale of Han action, the offensive of 97 BCE involved the use of about 210,000 troops. To act against the Xiongnu, the Han had to build up their cavalry, much of which, as with the Romans, was made up of allied forces; while reliance on conscription to raise a mass army was replaced by the build-up of a smaller professional force. The tension between the two forms of army has frequently played a role in military history.

However, the campaigns launched by Emperor Wuti (or Wudi), the 'Martial Emperor' (r. 140–87 BCE), who ceased paying subsidies to the Xiongnu confederation and, instead, launched repeated offensives, failed. Advancing into the vast distances to the north, the Han found it difficult to engage their opponents, and were soon obliged to retreat as supplies ran out. A few victories could not compensate for heavy costs in manpower and money, and it proved impossible to destroy the coherence of the Xiongnu. The policy of attack was replaced first by a defensive strategy and then by a peace that involved expensive gifts from the Han. Eventually, and a key demonstration of the significance of the political dimension, divisions among the Xiongnu provided the Han with allies. The Han were more successful in advancing to the south, gaining, for example, the regions of Nanyue (111 BCE) and Minyue (110 BCE) and this secured a southward migration of settlers that was of great importance in the reshaping of China.

The importance of war to the reputation of individual rulers was linked to the crucial role of military leadership and success in supporting royal status. This was the case in China, although war seems to have been less a part of Chinese ruling culture than it was further west. In Europe, leaders were expected to be able to fight, while war was crucial to the careers of many, often requiring their personal involvement in battle. This involvement is readily apparent with military leaders who grasped the imagination of contemporaries and later ages alike, such as Alexander the Great of Macedonia and Julius Caesar of Rome, and was also the case for lesser-known Roman emperors, who frequently launched campaigns merely to certify their right to the imperial purple.

The potentially decisive role of individual leadership and personality is brought out by Alexander the Great, ruler of Macedonia from 336 to 323 BCE, who used war to create a new political world spanning Macedonia, Greece, which had been brought under Macedonian hegemony by his father Philip, and the Persian Empire. Calling himself Lord of Asia, Alexander conquered the Persian Empire and then tried, for prudential reasons as well as a quasi-mystical sense of his own mission, to transform the rivalry of East and West, seen with the Greek perception of the Persian invasions of the previous century, into a new imperial unity. Alexander's goals and warfare took even further the new scale of conflict that the Persians had forced on the Greeks with the unsuccessful invasions that led to the Greek victories of Marathon (490 BCE), Salamis (480 BCE) and Plateae (479 BCE).

In the case of Alexander, this scale of conflict also led to the creation of a combined-arms army centred on effective heavy infantry (the disciplined phalanx of pikemen) with important cavalry support. This army brought Alexander successive victories over the Persians at the Granicus River (334 BCE), Issus (333 BCE) and Gaugamela. The last, fought on 1 October 331 BCE near Nineveh, was the decisive defeat of the Persian army. Alexander's force was 7,000 strong, that of the Persian ruler, Darius III, 40,000, although much of the latter were weak and poorly trained infantry who lacked the spirit of the battle-hardened Macedonians. Darius relied on his chariots and spearmen and he tended to direct the battle from a stationary centre. Alexander, in contrast, was primarily a cavalry general who led from the front. The Persian cavalry seriously pressed the Macedonians, but Alexander's cavalry itself hit the Persian left, and, with Darius apparently killed (in fact the chariot driver behind him was the victim), many of the Persians fled, destroying the cohesion of their centre.

In his influential history of Rome, Livy (Titus Livius *c.* 59 BCE–17 CE) considered what would have happened had Alexander, the greatest conqueror known to Antiquity, turned west and invaded Italy. Livy felt able to reassure his Roman readers that the might of Rome would have proved invincible. He commented on the quality of the Roman generalship of the age, and claimed that Alexander had become degenerate as a result of his absorption of Persian culture. Advancing a structural interpretation, Livy also contrasted the achievements of one man with those of a people in its 400th year of warfare. He argued, moreover, that Roman numbers, weaponry and fortifications were superior to those of Macedon, and that Rome was resilient and, in addition, as a sign of respective strengths, had subsequently defeated the Macedonians. Thus, Livy captured a key problem in military history: the balancing of individual circumstances, specifically Alexander's ability, and those that were more 'structural', in this case in the shape of Rome's military culture.

At the same time, the psychology of Rome's military culture was also important, notably the concern of its leaders with winning glory through war. Such glory, however, should not be seen as an irrational goal, as the resulting prestige helped ensure cohesion within the army, support within the empire and respect from those living beyond its bounds. War thus fed a positive image.

Alexander left no heir and his generals sought to carve realms for themselves, which is a frequent pattern in history and one that vied with that of generals as servants of the state. The armies of these Hellenistic rulers, notably the Antigonids, Seleucids and Ptolemies, all represented a continuation of Macedonian methods and an adoption of the troops they raised locally. Alexander's army indeed had come to include local troops, first as auxiliaries, but eventually in the infantry. There was a use of elephants, who in practice were more impressive than effective, although, in the hands of an experienced general, elephants could be much more than just a scare tactic. At Ipsos (301 BCE), the largest of the battles fought by Alexander's successors, the victorious Seleucus made good use of elephants, which frightened the horses of the opposing cavalry, and also probably employed horse archers. The Hellenistic armies, however, focused on the phalanx of pikemen, a formidable threat. Yet, the phalanx lacked flexibility and proved vulnerable to more mobile rivals, especially in broken terrain, a vulnerability that was to be exploited by the Romans, leading to the defeat of Macedonia in the second century BCE, notably at the Battle of Pydna in 168 BCE.

A personal involvement in campaigning was not simply true of would-be world conquerors such as Alexander. Roman politics was centrally intertwined with war. Politician-generals such as Crassus, Pompey and Julius Caesar regarded war as a way to win fame, money and a military base, and their ambitions helped drive Roman expansion in 67–52 BCE before leading in 49–46 BCE to a civil war between Pompey and Caesar; Crassus had been killed in 53 BCE in an unsuccessful attempt to conquer Parthia. Caesar defeated Pompey and declared himself dictator for life, but was assassinated in 44 BCE.

This personal involvement in campaigning was also the case with rulers and politicians who are not generally seen in that light, and that indicates the centrality of war. For example, Augustus, Caesar's adopted son and heir, campaigned against Mark Antony in 43 BCE, defeated Brutus and Cassius (the conspirators against Caesar) at the First and Second Battles of Philippi (42 BCE), overcame Mark Antony's brother, Lucius Antonius, at Perusia (41 BCE), campaigned in 40–36 BCE against Sextus Pompey, the son of Caesar's rival Pompey, pacified Dalmatia, Illyria and Pannonia (34 BCE), took a personal command role in Mark Antony's defeat at Actium (31 BCE), and, in 30 BCE, invaded Egypt, a key extension of Roman power, both politically and economically. Thus, the possibility of the delegation of military control did not preclude a direct role in war for leaders. The importance of command skills and also of appealing to the army were sufficient to affect the imperial succession. Thus the elderly Nerva (r. 96–8 CE), whose lack of military experience was a problem, adopted an experienced general, Trajan (r. 98–117 CE), as his son and successor. Earlier, the Praetorian Guard (imperial bodyguard), had forced the Senate to recognize Claudius (r. 41–54 CE) as Emperor, rather than restore the republic, and Claudius, in turn, invaded Britain in 43 CE in order to gain a military reputation and win popularity with the legions. His successor Nero's neglect of the army led to a rebellion in 68 CE that precipitated his fall.

Actium (31 BCE) was the key naval battle of the Roman world. At that stage, Augustus controlled the western part of the Roman Empire, including Italy, while his rival and former brother-in-law, Mark Antony, dominated the eastern part, supported by his new wife, Cleopatra VII, ruler of Egypt. Actium, on the western coast of Greece, was Mark Antony's anchorage, but it was a poor position because malaria weakened his forces, while their supply routes were endangered by Augustus's nearby troops, affecting morale and leading to desertions among the rowers. When part of Mark Antony's fleet tried to break out, it was defeated by that of Augustus. This defeat led Mark Antony to resolve to break out with the entire fleet. He was seriously outnumbered. In order to help break through the opposing centre and provide an opportunity for some of the warships to escape, as well as the merchantmen carrying his war chest, Mark Antony had the galleys on his wings move from the centre. He hoped this would lead his opponents to respond, weakening their centre. This tactic succeeded, enabling some of his fleet to break through and escape, but the abandonment of his army was a serious blow, and Augustus was able to press on to conquer Egypt, after both Mark Antony and Cleopatra committed suicide.

Modern full-scale reconstruction of triremes, a type of galley used for Classical warfare, has helped greatly in understanding the options faced by contemporary commanders. Galleys had rams on their prows, which could be used to devastating effect, but the preferred tactic was to bombard and board, employing catapults, archers and javelin-throwers to weaken resistance before trying to board. The necessity for considerable manpower to propel these vessels by rowing them greatly limited the cruising range of such ships, as they had to stop to take on more water and food. As a result, combined with the absence of living and sleeping quarters, galleys rarely abandoned the coastline and generally beached every night.

Like the Romans, the Hans faced instability as a result of their very own army as well as from the threat of invasions. While in Rome, Vespasian (r. 69–79 CE), an army commander, came to power after a civil war known as the Year of the Four Emperors, in China, after four decades of conflict between rival generals initially given command in order to suppress rebellions, the Han Emperor was forced to abdicate by one of the generals in 220 CE. Rival claimants led to the Age of the Three Kingdoms (200–65 CE), followed by the rule of the Western Jin dynasty which was unable to impose central control and which faced attack by the Xiongnu. In 311 CE, the latter stormed the Western Jin capital, Luoyang, wrecking the largest city in East Asia. The Xiongnu were effective cavalrymen, using both the light horse archer employed by other steppe peoples, and a heavy cavalry, armed with spear, sword and shield, able to close with infantry.

In addition, Turkic peoples overran much of north China by 500, establishing the Northern Wei dynasty (439–534). The Wei benefited from their control of the steppe which ensured plentiful horses and more cavalry there than their opponents. The Wei were also good at winning support from other groups, including from the far more numerous Chinese whom they ruled. Chinese administrative practices were adopted, and the Emperor Xiaowen (r. 471–99) created a hybrid regime with a sinicization of the Turkic Tuoba (Northern Wei) élite, prefiguring the policy of the Manchus in the seventeenth century (see pp. 80–4).

This process, however, was unacceptable to many of their soldiers, who were not sinicized, which led to rebellion. The Northern Wei state split and the Northern Zhou state was toppled by Yang Jian, a general, who founded the Sui dynasty (581–617), which went on to conquer the south. Armies from the steppe were able to deploy large numbers of skilled cavalry, but those from further south in China had limited access to horses and therefore lacked the mobility and offensive shock power of the northerners. The same pattern was true of India, while Western European militaries suffered from the greater ease of access to horses on the part of Eastern European forces.

This brief narrative will offer many echoes of those used in the standard account of Middle Eastern and Mediterranean warfare. The tension between settled societies and cavalry attackers, for example between the Seleucid Empire based in Persia and the eventually successful invading Parthian horse archers in about 280 BCE, was long-standing. Yet, this tension was also more complex than this description suggests, because of military co-operation across the border between settled and nomadic societies. The role of these 'barbarians' in the armies of settled societies indeed ensures that any account of Chinese or Roman military organization, or, indeed, that of many other empires, that offers a description of the core regulars is only partial. Instead, these powers deployed armies that were, in effect, coalition forces.

Such co-option could be structured essentially in two ways. It was possible to equip, train and organize ancillary forces in the same fashion as the core regulars, or to leave them to fight in a 'native' fashion. The net effect was a composite army, an organization that has been more common in military history than is generally allowed. The composite nature of large forces stemmed from the co-ordination of different armies. In imperial Rome, the native auxiliary units provided light cavalry and light infantry to assist the heavy infantry of the core Roman units, the legions, a professional force that replaced the earlier reliance on military service based on a property qualification. By the mid-first century CE, the *auxilia* contained over 200,000 men: a number larger than the legionaries. Granted citizenship on retirement, the auxiliaries also strengthened Rome politically. Most later imperial *auxilia* were heavily Romanized in equipment and fighting technique. They were hardly fighting in native fashion; just not in 'legionary' fashion.

Co-operation with 'barbarians' rested not so much on bureaucratic organization as on a careful politics of mutual advantage and an ability to create a sense of identification. Chinese relations with nomadic and semi-nomadic peoples of the steppe combined military force with a variety of diplomatic procedures, including *jimi* or 'loose rein', which permitted the incorporation of 'barbarian' groups into the Chinese realm. Their chiefs were given Chinese administrative titles, but continued to rule over their own people in traditional fashion, which assisted the policies of divide and rule that were important to the Chinese influence in the steppe. The Ottoman Turks were later to follow the same practices with the Albanian mountaineers.

This relationship with 'barbarians', both political and military, was also seen in the case of other empires. It was a relationship that was periodically to break down, most prominently with what was known as the 'barbarian' invasions, although that phrase runs together with and simplifies a lengthy and complex period of crisis. In the case of China, attacks by the Ruanruan (Avars), who had been a threat from the steppe in the sixth century, were followed by those from Turks. The impact of invasions was greater on India and the Roman Empire. Much of northern and central India had been united in the fourth century CE by the Gupta dynasty, but it was put under great pressure by invaders from Central Asia. The White Huns (Hephthalites) launched a major attack in 480, following up with more wide-ranging advances in the 500s and 510s. These greatly weakened Gupta power, preparing the way for the division of India from about 550 among a large number of regional powers, a division that lasted until the thirteenth century.

Sassanian-ruled Persia (the replacement in Persia from about 226 CE of the Parthian Empire) and the Eastern Roman Empire (Byzantium) both successfully resisted attack during this period. In contrast, the Western Roman Empire eventually succumbed to a series of assaults, Rome itself being sacked by the Visigoths under their ruler Alaric in 410 and the last Western Emperor being deposed in 476. The 'barbarian' invasions of Rome, however, were a complex process as some of the resistance was mounted by similar peoples: Germans made up much of the Roman field army in the fourth and, even more so, fifth centuries. There had been a major shift in Roman strategy under the pressure of increased attacks. The policy of strong frontier defence based on permanent border garrisons, which had been the norm from the late-first century CE to about 235 CE, as with Hadrian's Wall, was abandoned in favour of a defence in depth, relying on mobile field armies as the key element of a system that included fixed fortifications. The ostensible purpose of these field armies, in which cavalry played a greater role than hitherto, was to move out to meet invaders, but their primary function, however, often became the protection of the Emperor from internal rivals. This emphasis ensured that provinces were left susceptible to invasion, a process that sapped both resources and political support. The political role of the army was such that many of the emperors in the third century CE, for example Diocletian (r. 284–305) were Illyrian soldiers from the western Balkans, a region that was a major recruiting base for the army.

There were also changes in weaponry and tactics in the Roman army. A longer sword became predominant as part of a re-evaluation of fighting methods to cope with the 'barbarians'' armies. The longer sword came from the auxiliaries and was quite different from the Roman weapon as it was a cut-and-thrust weapon, unlike the classical Roman sword which was principally for stabbing and thus required less space to wield. The extent to which the Romans maintained their traditional formation of one main battle line, with the infantry in the centre flanked by cavalry and with a reserve in the rear, is unclear, but late Roman infantry was probably deployed as a phalanx. Moreover, the sophisticated infantry tactics of the Roman Republic (described in Polybius, Livy and Caesar), had long been abandoned. To a great extent, Roman battle formations, weaponry and tactics were not now the same as those of Republican Rome and the Early Empire (which began under Augustus). These alterations underline the extent to which military systems have the capacity for change, and it is therefore misleading to describe them in terms of an ideal form.

Key invasions of the Roman Empire were mounted by 'barbarian' groups pushed forward by the nomadic Huns, who, in turn, under Attila, invaded Western Europe. 'Barbarian' forces were not better armed, but they profited from determined leadership and from high morale. In one of the crucial battles, Adrianople (378), a terrible defeat in which the Goths destroyed a Roman army, killing the Emperor Valens, both sides used similar weapons. The Goths benefited instead from outnumbering the Romans. The Vandal conquest of the Maghrib (modern coastal Algeria and Tunisia) was a devastating blow as it was a key breadbasket for the Western Roman Empire.

Not all 'barbarians' employed cavalry, but many of the most effective raiders and conquerors were horsemen. The stirrup contributed to the potency of cavalry and was used by the Huns. The genesis of the stirrup was a long one, prefiguring the later situation with gunpowder (see pp. 49–50). It is possible that the Scythians used leather loops in the fourth century BCE, although these may simply have been to help in mounting the horse. These loops were not, therefore, able to provide a better fighting platform, which, instead, was offered by the use of rigid metal stirrups. Stirrups were an improvement, but only an incremental one. The horse had been used effectively in warfare long before stirrups were developed, and many of the features noted in cavalry warfare with stirrups had been anticipated earlier. Stirrups, nevertheless, provided stability in motion, helping in both shock action and with firing projectiles from horseback; in other words assisting both heavy and light cavalry. These actions did not depend on stirrups, but stirrups helped make them more effective. The earliest Chinese figurine with two stirrups probably dates from about 322 CE.

The fall of Rome did not mark the end of the 'barbarian' invasions, although there was also resistance, and, on occasion, the driving back of the 'barbarians'. Most dramatically, the potential represented by the Byzantine (Eastern Rome) development of the later-Roman army was revealed in the Byzantine recapture of North Africa, Italy and the south coast of Spain in 533–51 from the 'barbarian' kingdoms of the Vandals, Ostrogoths and Visigoths respectively. These campaigns, in which the key general was Belisarius, revealed the need for an extensive range of skills. Amphibious capability was a prerequisite for the Byzantine campaigns, while siegecraft was also necessary, as shown by the capture of Palermo (535) and Ravenna (539). Victory in battle required the ability to gain the initiative and to maintain pressure on the enemy, as demonstrated against the Vandals at Tricamerum (533), a struggle decided by Byzantine cavalry charges.

The sparse nature of the sources is such that much of the conflict in Europe in the fifth to tenth centuries is obscure, as, more seriously, are the reasons for military capability and the nature of developments. In particular, the dating and extent of the rise of heavy cavalry, the basis of the later medieval knight, is unclear. Traditional interpretations that this rise was due to the diffusion of the stirrup, which provided greater stability, and to the Christian response to Muslim cavalry, have been called into question. It has been argued, instead, that cavalry was important throughout, an important aspect of a continuity from the Roman Empire that is more generally debated; but also that the mass 'shock charge' of heavy cavalry only became important from the eleventh century.

Meanwhile 'barbarian' attacks continued on Byzantium and on the successor states to the Roman Empire. The Lombards overran much of northern Italy from 568, while the Angles and Saxons had won control of most of England by the close of the seventh century, despite the efforts of Romano-British leaders such as Arthur. The Vikings and Magyars were to mount major attacks in the ninth and tenth centuries, with Christendom under pressure from both sea and land, but, by then, much of the Eurasian world had been transformed by the advance of Islam.

From the Creation of the Islamic World to the Start of European Transoceanic Expansion, 630–1490

Launched by Muhammad, the advance of Islam demonstrated the role of ideology in helping explain conflict and in playing a role in success. The new religion rapidly involved conflict with the paganism that prevailed in most of Arabia. Muhammad defeated opposing forces in 624 and 627, and captured Mecca in 630. His successors, known as caliphs, Abu Bakr (r. 632–4), 'Uman (r. 634–44) and 'Uthman (r. 644–58), presided over a tremendous expansionism that involved the defeat of Byzantium (the Eastern Roman Empire) and the overthrow of Sassanian Persia. First, Arabia was united. Then the Byzantines were defeated at Yarmuk and the Persians at Al Qadisiya, both probably in 636. Earlier conflicts between the two powers wore them down and helped give the Arabs an edge. These victories were partly due to the impact of the Arab archers, although the nature of the surviving sources is such that it is difficult to make accurate comments about force structure, size, weapons and tactics. Early Arab armies were not dominated by cavalry, as the Arabs had very few horses. Instead, warriors fought dismounted.

Syria and Mesopotamia were conquered by the Arabs, followed, in 639–41, by Egypt, with victory at Heliopolis in 640 proving crucial. The Byzantine defenders of Egypt, only 25–30,000 strong, were poorly commanded and many of the local levies were of low quality. But the invading army was smaller, only about 15,500 strong. The dynamic of the Byzantine defensive position had been wrecked by the loss of Syria, as that ensured that the other regions were unable to support one another. Moreover, the Byzantines were unable to mount a riposte comparable to that, for example, which eventually followed the defeat and capture of the Roman Emperor Valerian at Edessa in 260 by the Sassanian ruler, Shapur, a defeat that initially led to a crisis in the Roman east.

The Arabs also advanced into Persia, routing the Sassanians at Nehavend (642) and capturing Herat in modern Afghanistan (650). Other Arab forces advanced into Anatolia (in modern Turkey) in 644 and across North Africa, capturing Tripoli, the capital of modern Libya. With them, the Arabs brought the bridle and stirrup to North Africa, which helped to make the Arab cavalry particularly effective. More generally, the Arab forces appear to have benefited from mobility and morale, rather than numbers. The Arab ability to win over non-Arab troops to their side was of crucial importance, especially during the conquest of Iraq, and this was a capability that brought more manpower and also new military techniques.

Religious enthusiasm rooted in Islam helped to give this series of attacks greater cohesion, as well as range, than those of other 'barbarian' invaders, although, as a sign of the breakdown of cohesion, the caliphate itself was disputed from the 650s. Nevertheless, under the Umayyad caliphs (661–750), the process of expansion continued. The remainder of the Mediterranean coast of North Africa was overrun and, in 711, the Berber general Tariq led 7,000 troops across the Straits of Gibraltar. The Visigoths, who ruled Iberia (Spain and Portugal), were divided and suffered greatly from a lack of support among their subjects. At the Guadelette River (711), Tariq defeated and killed the Visigoth king Roderic, winning another battle at Ecija later that year. Most of Iberia was then rapidly conquered, and the Arabs crossed the Pyrenees into modern France. At the other geographical extreme, there was expansion to the River Indus in modern Pakistan. More generally, Arab armies became more professional under the Umayyads, with greater tactical sophistication linked to organizational flexibility.

There were also, however, checks. Sieges of the Byzantine capital, Constantinople (now Istanbul), in 668–75 and 716–18 crucially failed, while, in 732, the Franks under Charles Martel defeated an Arab army at Poitiers. The historian Edward Gibbon was to write in the late-eighteenth century that, had the Arabs won, it might have led to the conquest of Christian Europe:

> A victorious line of march had been prolonged above a thousand miles from the rock of Gibraltar to the banks of the Loire; the repetition of an equal space would have carried the Saracens to the confines of Poland and the Highlands of Scotland: the Rhine is not more impassable than the Nile or the Euphrates.

Recent analysis is more sceptical, but also indicates the difficulty of arriving at conclusions. For example, it has been argued that the Arab expedition was simply a raid but also that it was important as the Arab force was substantial and that its victory could have reinforced the pattern of Christian co-operation with the Arabs which, in turn, would have helped the latter maintain a strong presence in France. As with many battles, Poitiers was more significant for one side (the Franks) than the other. At any rate, the Arabs, although they had a base at Fraxinetum in Provence in southern France from 890 to 972, never repeated their advance so far north in France.

Nineteen years after Poitiers, in 751, as a potent sign of the range of Muslim power, an Arab army under Ziyad bin Salih, Governor of Samarkand, defeated a Chinese counterpart under Gao Xianzhi at Atlakh near Lake Balkhash. This helped to ensure that the expansion of the Jang dynasty into western Turkestan was halted and, instead, drove forward a process of Islamicization in Central Asia. The battle was decided when an allied contingent of Qarluq Turks abandoned Gao and defected to Ziyad. This, however, was the sole major battle between Chinese and Arab armies, as the Arabs made no effort to press east into the Tarim Basin and Xinjiang.

The previous year, 750, in the Battle of the Zab at Tell Kushaf in Iraq, Umayyad power was overcome by the outnumbered Abbasids, who claimed descent from the uncle of Muhammad. The Abbasid rebellion had started in Persia in 747 and the rebels captured Baghdad in 749 and Damascus in 750. The Battle of the Zab serves as a reminder of the extent to which militaries thought of in terms of single weapons systems and tactics, in this case Arabs and cavalry, were often more varied. In the battle, the dismounted Abbasids formed a spearwall from behind which their archers fired. Alongside infantry and light cavalry, the Abbasid caliphs (750–1258) relied on armoured heavy cavalry armed with swords, clubs and axes, although they devoted far less attention to expansion than the Umayyads had done. As with the Romans, the Abbasids co-opted those they thought barbarians, but their imported Turkish slaves (who became *ghulam* or slave soldiers) became a source of instability. At the same time, these slave soldiers reduced Abbasid dependence on the Arab military aristocracy, much of whom had proved politically unreliable. Muslim armies took a variety of forms, but a key component in some were professional slave soldiers. This, for example, was the case in Moorish Spain in the ninth century, and the force there grew to about 60,000 strong.

Although the Abbasid Empire was wide-ranging, the Muslim world was fractured, and increasingly so with rebellions, civil wars and invasions framing much of the narrative of Muslim military history after their initial expansion in the eighth century. For example, in Spain, the Berber settlers from North Africa, who were treated as second-class subjects by the ruling Arabs, rebelled in 740, which gave the Christians in northern Spain a breathing space. This rebellion was to be followed in the ninth century in Spain by those of Muslim converts, who were also treated as second-class subjects. In 756, Muslim Spain had become independent from the caliphate, remaining thereafter a centre of Umayyad power: a member of the Umayyad family overthrew the unpopular Abbasid governor of Spain, ending the political unity of the Muslim world, although the strength of the latter aspiration was shown with the attempt to restore Umayyad control of the caliphate. There was further fracturing of the Muslim world thereafter. For example, the Shi'ite Fatimids established a caliphate in Tunis in 910 and, from there, conquered Egypt in 969, while the Seljuk Turks captured Baghdad in 1055.

Muslim divisions did not prevent fresh expansion, including, in the ninth century, the conquest of Sicily, Sardinia and Malta. Yet, these divisions provided a crucial opportunity for Christendom, both by lessening the pressure on it, and by enabling the Christians to capture part of Spain in 1030–85, Sicily in 1061–93 and, in the Crusades, much of modern Syria, Lebanon, Israel and Palestine in the 1090s and the early-twelfth century. The First Crusade, spurred on by the ambition of retaking the holy city of Jerusalem, fulfilled its goal in 1099. Initial gains along the coast of modern Syria, Lebanon and Israel were expanded with the capture of Tyre (1124) and Ascalon (1153), although, launched in response to the loss of Edessa, one of the Crusader states, in 1144, the Second Crusade failed to capture Damascus in 1148. The Crusades also inspired a novel form of monastic organization, the Military Orders: the Templars and Hospitallers had troops and castles and were entrusted with the defence of large tracts of territory.

However, despite the construction of impressive castles, such as Belvoir and Krak des Chevaliers, the Crusaders found it difficult to sustain their presence, being placed under particular pressure by Saladin. He founded the Ayymbia sultanate in Egypt in 1171, before conquering Syria and, in 1187, smashing the Crusaders of the kingdom of Jerusalem at Hattin, a defeat of heavy cavalry by well-deployed and more flexible light cavalry. Similarly, the Christians in Spain were put under pressure when the Muslims there turned for support to the Almoravids, Saharan Berbers who had overrun Morocco in the 1060s. In 1086, the Almoravids defeated Alfonso of Castile at Sagrajas, and in 1102 recaptured the city of Valencia. As a result, a temporary end was put to the Christian offensive in Spain.

In a reminder of variety, the Crusaders, who enjoyed a degree of recovery in the Middle East, recapturing the fortress of Acre and defeating Saladin at Arsun, both in 1191, during the Third Crusade; nevertheless, lost their last position there, Acre, to the Mamelukes in 1291. In contrast, in Spain and Portugal, there was a recovery of the initiative by the Christians, notably in the 1140s. The Almohads from Morocco lent new energy to the Muslim resistance thereafter, smashing the Spanish Castilians at Alarcos in 1195, but they were crushed in a surprise attack at the Battle of Las Navas de Tolosa in 1212. Most of southern Spain was overrun by Castilians by 1275. The kingdom of Granada, the last Muslim principality in Spain, finally followed in 1492, a conquest that reflected Granadan divisions as much as the strengths of the Castilian military, including cannon, but with effective infantry also important.

As a further reminder of the extent and variety of conflict between Christendom and Islam, the Holy Roman Emperor Frederick II bloodily suppressed a Muslim rebellion in Sicily. This had begun in 1189 and left the mountainous interior of the island in practice an independent state that both resisted the Christians and sought help from Muslim powers elsewhere. Between 1220 and 1246, Frederick launched a series of campaigns which destroyed the Muslim community of Sicily. Malta had been conquered in an expedition sent from Sicily in 1127.

The impact of the Muslim advances helped not only to mould the modern world, but also indicated the vulnerability of settled agricultural societies to attacks from the desert and steppe. This vulnerability was to be demonstrated repeatedly over the millennium beginning with the Arab advances, and most prominently by the nemesis of the Abbasids, the Mongols. The Mongols also followed and, in 1234, overcame the Jurchen, who had already displayed, the previous century, the potential of steppe forces by conquering the Khitan who ruled northern China and pressing hard the Sung who were driven back into the south. In the thirteenth century, the Mongols overran China and advanced as far as Hungary, Syria, Java and Japan, in an effort to conquer and unify the world known to them.

Affected by a subsistence crisis in the steppe that in part arose from a temperature drop that affected grass growth, the Mongols looted and then took over large parts of the world of settled agriculture. Their success offered an important indication of military capability with mounted archers, providing mobility and firepower, being organized in a coherent military system that was able to respond to challenges, adapting most obviously to the need to capture Chinese cities, as well as to that for a navy. Their success was particularly impressive as the Mongols operated in a range of environments.

The Europeans were never able to defeat the Mongols, and were lucky that Chinggis Khan, the great Mongol leader, concentrated on China and then the Muslim states of Central Asia. However, the successful Mongol campaign against the Khwarizm Shah of Persia (1220–1) led Mongol forces to move west across the Caucasus, defeating the kingdom of Georgia, as well as the nomadic Alans and Cumans to the north of the Caucasus, and the south Russian princes. Achieved by a subsidiary Mongol force, this advance indicated the vulnerability of Europe to the mobile peoples of Central Asia. The Mongols returned in 1236 under Batu, a grandson of Chinggis Khan, reputedly at the head of 120,000 men. The northern principalities of Rus were overrun in 1237–9, while the city of Kiev was stormed and razed in 1240. At Liegnitz (1241), the horns of the deployment of the more numerous Mongol army outflanked their German-Polish opponents, who were hard hit from the flanks by Mongol mounted archers. This rout was followed by the destruction, by the main Mongol force invading Europe, of the Hungarian army at Mohi.

The Mongols only turned back when news arrived that the Great Khan was dead. In contrast to this lack of defeat, another Mongol army, having captured the key Syrian cities of Aleppo and Damascus in 1259, was defeated at Ayn Jalut (1260) by the Mamelukes of Egypt, with their mounted archers. Such limits were important to world history. Thus, the loss (largely due to a storm) of the Mongol invasion fleet at Hakata Bay (1281) ensured that Japan, unlike Korea, would remain outside the orbit of China, which was then ruled by the

Mongols. An earlier attempt on Japan had been wrecked by a storm in 1274. The Mamelukes, originally slave-soldiers from Central Asia, were also effective in using their cavalry as shock troops, and were adept at siege warfare. Any stress on Mongol limits elsewhere has to be considered, however, alongside the Mongol need to devote major resources for a long period to the conquest of China where Sung power was not finally destroyed until 1279.

The Mongol Empire was a particularly potent cavalry-based empire. The strength of such empires was in part due to the potential of horsemen, especially with stirrups, deeper saddles and new horse tack, which improved both their stability and their manoeuvrability, but factors of organization and leadership were also crucially important. These factors were not only the case in explaining why non-steppe forces could be overcome but also in accounting for whichever cavalry-based empire triumphed, a question that could not be so readily explained in terms of technology.

In turn, as earlier with the fates of the empires of Alexander the Great and the creators of the Macedonian and Carolingian Empires, the Mongol inheritance was divided, with the successor states continuing the military methods although also adapting them to specific tasks and opportunities. The fourteenth century was an age of decline for the Mongols due in part to lost impetus and in part to rivalries among them. Having effectively controlled or threatened much of Eurasia in the thirteenth century, the withdrawal and decay of the Mongols in the fourteenth (in which the Mongols were driven from China in 1368) was a major factor in the subsequent military history of Eurasia, as no future steppe force matched their sustained drive.

The most impressive subsequent steppe force was very much limited to the reign of one individual, Timur the Lame (1336–1405; later called Tamerlane). Claiming descent from Chinggis Khan, whose dream of world domination he revived, and modelling himself on the Mongols, Timur campaigned widely. The cities he captured included Delhi, Baghdad and Damascus, a success that was not to be repeated until the British held all three (two only very briefly) at the close of the First World War. In 1402, at Ankara, Timur defeated and captured the Ottoman (Turkish) sultan, Bayazid I, a key achievement in what turned out to be a short-term consolidation of Muslim power in Timur's person. At the time of his death, Timur was planning to invade China, where the rule of the Ming dynasty had been established in 1368.

The nomadic empires and their light cavalry were, like the Arab armies of early Islam, difficult to stop militarily, but they proved less successful in maintaining control over large settled agrarian regions. In part, this was a matter of contingency and of the nature of their opponents, but the Mongols and, Timur in particular, suffered from a lack of legitimating principles and from the resulting problems of political cohesion in their empires.

In Europe, in contrast, there was greater success in creating and sustaining such legitimation, but generally only for relatively small-scale polities rather than far-flung empires. The Franks under Charlemagne (r. 771–814), the founder of the Carolingian Empire, were able to conquer and unite most of Western Christendom, crucially uniting most of modern France, Germany and Italy, but this territorial achievement was divided among his grandsons. Thereafter, such a territorial scope was repeated in Europe only by Napoleon and Hitler, and then only briefly in large part because it did not strike contemporaries as legitimate. The smaller-scale states of Western Christendom displayed a range of military forms and, like the situation elsewhere in the world, there was, alongside the needs of warmaking, a correspondence between such forms and social structures. As a key development, the kingdoms of Western Europe, from the late-ninth century, found their authority challenged by local potentates who were to create feudal domains, producing a new political system with a clear military counterpart, including private unlicensed castles. Vassals (sworn followers) were given land in return for providing military service, usually in the form of knights: heavy (armoured) cavalry, although in Spain there were *caballeros villanos*, knights who were non-noble and were expected to farm themselves.

Yet, it is also important to note the range of the medieval military system. Although trained to fight while mounted, knights, who were all-purpose warriors, frequently dismounted for combat, as did their Japanese counterparts. Moreover, the absence of horses from the New World, from rainforest Africa, from the New World (the Americas) and from Australasia ensured that the socially and politically prominent fought on foot there. In Europe, there were also many soldiers who were not knights. Infantry played a major role in siegecraft and the defence of castles (the key defensive positions), and also an important part in battle. Similarly, alongside the long-established Byzantine emphasis on heavy cavalry and on the tactics of a shock-delivery wedge, the Byzantine armies came to put a greater stress on infantry and light cavalry from the tenth century.

Warfare and political success were closely linked to the quality of leadership. Command in the medieval period was generally synonymous with rulership, because the willingness and ability to lead into battle were seen as crucial attributes of a ruler. Thus, Abd al-Rahman III (891–961), the Emir of Moorish Spain from 912, felt able as a result of victories to declare himself Caliph of Córdoba in 929, taking, at the same, time, the title al-Nasir li-Dini Allah, 'he who fights victoriously for the faith of God'. However, at Simancas in 939, Abd al-Rahman was heavily defeated by Ramiro II of Léon and he never thereafter led a campaign in person.

This perception of military success as crucial to rulership caused serious problems if the monarch was unable to lead or was judged to be unable to provide adequate military leadership. The contrast was readily apparent with the kings of England. Richard I, Edward I, Edward III and Henry V were great warleaders who won prestige through conflict, while Edward II and Henry VI proved cruelly disappointing in this light, losing the English positions in Scotland and France respectively. Moreover, each was to be overthrown and murdered.

Gains made through war brought rulers and their dynasties to the fore. If the most spectacular were the cases of Chinggis Khan, Saladin and Timur, the same process was true at a more modest level. While the successors of Alfred the Great, especially Athelstan, established the Old English state by defeating the Danes in the late-ninth and early-tenth centuries, unifying England for the first time since the Romans; Sweyn and Cnut of Denmark, in turn, established Danish rule over England in the early-eleventh century, in what was a very different type of operation to the Viking raids of the early-eighth century. The Old England dynasty returned peacefully in 1042, in the person of Edward the Confessor, but in 1066 Duke William of Normandy became William the Conqueror thanks not only to his total victory over King Harold at Hastings, but also to the successful exploitation of it which led to him becoming William I of England.

Leadership, therefore, entailed not only success in battle but also the ability to derive political benefits from campaigning. This ability was a matter not only of directing and sustaining the coalitions of support that rulers depended on when leading clan heads, aristocrats, subordinates and allies, but also ensuring that opponents accepted the verdict of defeat and transferred their loyalty. This situation could entail taking over new roles as leader, as when Charlemagne became Holy Roman Emperor in 800, laying claim to the legacy of Rome and also enshrining a new alliance with the Papacy, or when the Mongols established themselves on the throne of China in the thirteenth century. An understanding of political possibilities and of how best to translate campaign successes into permanent advantage proved crucial to military leadership. As with prowess on the battlefield, the emphasis was on the individual. He could not rely on subordinates nor on a staff. It was the ruler who had to prove himself as the leader.

The death of a strong leader could easily lead to political collapse. The death in 1002 of al-Mansur, who had effectively ruled the Muslim Caliphate of Cordova since 981 and achieved many successes at the expense of the Christians, was followed by the fragmentation of Muslim Spain, which provided the Christians with a crucial advantage. A strong leader, by contrast, could rapidly restore the fortunes of a state. The Byzantine Emperor Basil II (r. 976–1025), for example, destroyed the West Bulgarian Empire (1018), a bitter rival to Byzantium, and reduced the Serbs to vassalage. He gained his surname 'Bulgar-slayer' from the Battle of the Belasica Mountains (1014) after which thousands of prisoners were blinded and sent home in groups of ten, each led by a one-eyed man.

In contrast, under Basil's successors, the previously successful Byzantine military machine found itself starved of funds, and a much weakened Byzantine army was defeated by the Seljuk Turks at Manzikert in 1071. The defeat was followed by the loss of almost all Anatolia to the Seljuks and this proved an important background to the sense of Muslim menace to Christendom that encouraged the calling of the First Crusade by Pope Urban II in 1095.

In Western Europe, the emphasis in war was on capturing castles and towns and on devastating territories, whereas the frequency of battles varied. Castles were inhabited, rather than places of refuge, unlike the hill forts which had been numerous in the Iron Age. Early castles were generally simple affairs of earth and timber construction, although they still required many man-days to construct. Timber-built forms were often of either motte (a mound of earth)-and-bailey or ringwork (enclosure) type, both of which had long currency into the thirteenth century. Not all castles were built of timber and earthwork. There was also construction in stone which, crucially, was resistant to fire and therefore was better able to repel attack. Cost and the shortage of skilled masons were issues, but, with time, major castles were fortified in stone.

Castles provided a means to extend power, both to ensure domestic control and on frontiers, for example those of Christendom. There were also non-Christian traditions of castle building, including in Japan and by Arab rulers. In China, the emphasis was on city walls, and they were relatively low, extremely thick and made of packed earth, rather than the brittle stone which made European fortresses vulnerable, whether to stones thrown by trebuchets, to ramming, to mining or, eventually, to cannon.

Despite the importance of sieges, there were major battles in Western Europe. Moreover, armies had always to be ready for battle. The key importance of battles was demonstrated for example by Tinchebrai in 1106, which ended the challenge to the unity of the Norman succession in the person of Henry I of England (son of William the Conqueror) posed by the claims of his eldest brother, Robert.

Knights did not always prevail in Western Europe, not least because they were of limited tactical value in capturing fortresses. Moreover, some infantry armies were able to defeat those focused on knights, whether mounted or not. This shift is sometimes considered in terms of the rise of missile weapons – first the longbow and then firearms; but infantry forces armed with stabbing and thrusting weapons, such as spears and pikes, were also victorious. Key instances included the infantry of the Lombard League in north Italy in the twelfth century, which defeated the Holy Roman Emperors Frederick Barbarossa at Legnano in 1176 and Frederick II at Parma in 1248, the Scots in the 1290s–1310s at the expense of the English, notably at Stirling (1296) and Bannockburn (1314), and the infantry of both Flanders and the Swiss Cantons in the early-fourteenth century. The former defeated the French, while Habsburg forces were defeated by the Swiss at Morgarten (1315) and Zug (1386). Similarly, the knights of the German crusading orders in the eastern Baltic, the Knights of the Sword and the Teutonic Knights, could be defeated, for example by the Lithuanians at Durben in 1260 and Tannenburg in 1410, while the Mongols were driven from China in 1368.

The infantry challenge was greatly enhanced with the English development of a longbow capability in the fourteenth century. The longbowmen played a key role in defeating the Scots at Halidon Hill (1333), and the French at Crécy (1346) and Poitiers (1356), and in helping John of Avis defeat a Castilian invasion of Portugal at Aljubarrota (1385), a key step in maintaining Portuguese independence. These longbowmen lacked the operational and tactical flexibility of Central Asian archers because they could not fire from the saddle and tended to fight on the defensive. This was a major limitation as, like most other infantry forces in this period, the longbowmen depended on being attacked. Partly as a result, in what would be subsequently termed the Hundred Years' War with France, the English rulers found themselves unable to translate their victories into permanent success. This situation again proved the pattern in the early-fifteenth century, with Henry V victorious at Agincourt in 1415 over attacking French forces brought low by English arrows; but his successor's generals were unable to prevent a French revival.

If technology was one of the drivers of military change, another was provided by developments in organization and in the political context. For example, the intensity of the conflict in which Edward I of England became involved in the mid-1290s, war with both France and Scotland, led to unprecedented financial demands. These result-ed in political changes, notably the development of Parliament, the creation of a tax state and challenges to the Crown's authority. In turn, these changes affected the political parameters in England within which choices could be made about war and how best to pursue it.

The possibilities of naval warfare were constrained by the tech-nological limitations of ships, dominated as they were by the pressures of wind and wave and without the possibilities that were subsequently to be offered by cannon and, later, steam power. Furthermore, most states were ruled by monarchs and élites who focused on landed values and land conflict. Nevertheless, it would be mistaken to imagine that there was no naval conflict nor related command skills. In some cases, moreover, the ability to move troops across the sea was important. This was the case with the Vikings, including the Danish invasions of England in the ninth and eleventh centuries, with the Norman invasion of England in 1066, with the Crusades and with the two unsuccessful Mongol invasions of Japan, as well as the attack on Java in 1292–3. Naval actions in northern European waters were largely fought from the mid-fourteenth century by sailing ships, although galley fleets continued to play a key role in the Mediterranean.

Chinggis Khan and Timur, the two commanders whose forces ranged the furthest afield, did not need to use oceanic navies, although the Mongols did create an effective river navy in order to help overcome the use of defensive river lines by the Southern Sung. Moreover, his successors mounted amphibious attacks on Japan and Java. The steppe across which Chinggis Khan and Timur operated was in some respects land oceans: large and difficult areas across which they had to advance. Their forces were particularly well attuned to this combat environment. As so often, success in command was in large part a matter of the adroit exploitation of possibilities, and successful command therefore was an aspect of the strengths of the general military culture and environment.

This combination was seen in the eventual result of the Hundred Years' War between England and France. The English political failure in France, in being unable to end opposition and establish the legitimacy and acceptability of Henry VI's claim to the French throne, was finally matched by one in weaponry, as the French deployed an impressive train of artillery in 1449–51. Gunpowder weaponry had been developed in China, where effective metal-barrelled weapons were produced in the twelfth century. This development owed much to the intensity of warfare in China in the twelfth and thirteenth centuries, as Jurchen and then Mongol armies attacked the Sung. This intensity led to pressure for the development of new weaponry, not least incendiary and explosive devices. Sung innovations were rapidly adopted by the steppe powers, as a result of the use of defectors and mercenaries, as well as the capture of artisans and weapons, each a key means for the diffusion of military technology. The Jurchen, indeed, oversaw the production of the first iron-cased explosives or bombs, which were used in a siege in 1221, although hand grenades probably date back to the tenth century. At the same time, gunpowder weaponry was not seen as the only solution. Thus, the Mongols also devoted attention not only to bowmen but also to copying large Persian (counter-weighted) catapults. These, not cannon, played the key role in ending the difficult siege of the Chinese city of Hsiang-yang (1267–73).

Knowledge of gunpowder was brought from China to Europe in the mid-thirteenth century. Weapons that employed gunpowder also spread from China, not only cannon but also, eventually, grenades (fifteenth century) and rockets (late-eighteenth century via India). Gunpowder weapons came into frequent use in Europe from the early-fourteenth century. Gunpowder, however, posed serious problems if its potential as a source of energy was to be utilized effectively. For a long period, cannon were not strong enough to make proper use of gunpowder, but, in around 1420, 'corned' powder was developed, providing the necessary energy but without dangerously high peak pressures which could damage the gun. More powerful artillery required better guns, which were provided by advances in wrought-iron gun manufacture. Moreover, the effectiveness of artillery was increased by the replacement of stone by iron cannon balls, by improvements in the transport of cannon and by the development of the trunnion which made it easier to change the angle of fire. Hand-held gunpowder weapons also became increasingly important during the fifteenth century. Gunpowder, therefore, was not a one-stage invention. Instead, like most inventions, it involved a complex process of development.

French cannon helped bring the speedy fall of English-held fortified positions in France in 1449–51, in marked contrast with the time taken in many earlier sieges, such as the English sieges of Calais (successful, 1346–7) and Orléans (unsuccessful, 1428–9). Other rulers, such as the Dukes of Burgundy, built up a large artillery park, the cannon being used to breach the walls of rebellious towns. More dramatically, Constantinople had successfully resisted sieges by 'barbarian' non-Western powers for centuries (although it fell to the Fourth Crusade in 1204), but, in 1453, it fell to an Ottoman army that had employed cannon to breach its walls. This fall inflicted a bitter psychological blow on Christendom and signalled the extent to which war could dramatically alter the political order. The Eastern Roman Empire was reduced to fragments that would soon fall.

The path from the breaching of the walls of Constantinople to the present day may seem clear, with enhanced firepower progressively changing the character of battle while also driving up the costs of war, encouraging its monopolization at the more sophisticated level by states able to afford it. Yet, this was a course that in practice was far from clear, and it is especially pertinent to note the variety of military circumstances and means of warmaking in the mid-fifteenth century, a variety that can also be noted today. At Tumu in 1449, the Yingzong Emperor of China was captured and his army destroyed in a Mongol ambush. This defeat brought to an end the pattern of Chinese offensives against the Mongols and, instead, encouraged Chinese reliance on a defensive strategy based on walls.

In Europe, also, it was unclear that enhanced firepower would change the nature of war. Instead, there was an emphasis on horse archers in Muscovy, and on cavalry in the French and Burgundian armies, while Swiss pikemen acquired a formidable reputation in the late-fifteenth century, routing Charles the Bold of Burgundy at Grandson, Murten and Nancy in 1476–7. The disciplined drill did not rely on individual courage. To Clausewitz, in *On War* (1832), these Swiss successes afforded the 'first and strongest demonstration of the superiority of good infantry against the best cavalry'.

Similarly, on the oceans. It is easy to chart a course from Portuguese exploration, trade and settlement, south along the African coast and into the islands of the eastern Atlantic in the early-fifteenth century, to later European dominance of the oceans. In fact, in the early-fifteenth century, the Chinese were more wide-ranging at sea. Carrying cannon possibly from the 1350s, they were able to send fleets into the Indian Ocean, where Sri Lanka was successfully invaded in 1411. If the situation was different by 1490, this difference was due not to any defeat of the Chinese fleet by Western naval forces, for none occurred, but, rather, to a shift in Chinese priorities away from oceanic expansion and towards confrontation with the Mongols.

In the meanwhile, the inexorable advance of the Ottoman Turks appeared to be a stark demonstration of European weakness. The Ottoman state originated as a frontier principality in the Byzantine–Seljuk frontier zone in north-western Anatolia. In the fourteenth century, the Ottomans became an important power on either side of the Sea of Marmara, in 1361 capturing Adrianople (Edirne) to where they moved their capital in 1402. The Christians seemed powerless in the face of the relentless tide of their advance and Bulgaria succumbed rapidly. In 1385 Sofia fell to the Turks, and in 1386 Nish. In 1389, the Serbian army of King Lazar was defeated by the Ottomans at Kosovo, breaking the back of Serbia's resistance. Serbia and Wallachia became Ottoman vassal states, Constantinople was blockaded and Thessaly in Greece was conquered. In 1396, a Hungarian-French crusade sent to relieve the Byzantines was destroyed at Nicopolis on the Danube. The remaining fragments of Byzantium were only saved by the far greater success of Timur in crushing the Ottomans near Ankara in 1402, just as, earlier, in the late-thirteenth century, Mongol victories over their Arab opponents had delayed the fall of the surviving Crusader positions in the Middle East. Conversely, Mameluke successes against the Mongols provided the opportunity for eventually taking these positions.

Similarly, Murad II restored the Ottoman position and the danger posed by Ottoman encroachments grew so great that in 1443 a crusade set out under the leadership of Wladislas I of Hungary (Wladyslaw III of Poland). Initially, the crusaders captured Nish and Sofia, and in 1444 Wladislas advanced as far as Varna on the Black Sea, but he was routed and killed there by Murad II. His successor, Mehmet II, not only captured Constantinople, but also the Morea (Pelopennese), the remainder of Serbia and some of the Aegean islands. With the capture of the city of Trebizond in 1461, the last remnant of Byzantium was finally extinguished. In the Balkans, the

Ottoman siege of Belgrade in 1456 was raised, but it seemed apparent that Europe faced a new series of invasions that it might not survive. Indeed, in 1480, Ottoman forces landed at Otranto in southern Italy, within campaigning distance of Rome. The Western Roman Empire has been extinguished just over a millennium earlier, and a new conquest of Western Europe appeared imminent.

The Gunpowder Empires of the Early-Modern World, 1490–1630

The focus for change for this period moves from the mounted archers of the Eurasian steppe to the European navigators of the oceans, but this is a priority that has to be hedged with caveats. It would have surprised the Ming Emperors of China (1368–1644) or their Mughal counterparts in India to have been told that the small European ships that periodically appeared off their coasts were the key military movers of the age or the harbingers of a new order. Indeed, the military history of much of the world can be told without reference to European warships, and this was to be dramatized in the mid-seventeenth century when Manchu invaders overthrew Ming China which proved the most significant political shift of the century and the one involving most troops. Nevertheless, for the Americas and for coastal societies in Africa and South Asia, European transoceanic expansion was of great importance, as it also was for the future history of the world as a whole. This situation invites the questions not only of why the West became so successful at such force projection, but also why it was not matched by other powers, either in the type of naval strength or in its use.

Technical explanations play a role, especially with reference to Western methods of construction, gunfounding and navigation. In each case, the application of knowledge proved valuable, as part of an active system of problem-solving in which the authority of the past was of limited sway. Yet, such explanations have to be set within a context of a Western willingness to invest in such shipping and as part of an expensive maritime and naval infrastructure. This willingness in part reflected the availability of merchant investment, as well as the extent to which merchant groups, such as the Dutch and English East India Companies, were able to devise and pursue policies, both on their own account and within the formal mechanism of the state in so far as the latter abstraction has much meaning for this period. Conversely, merchant groups did not enjoy these freedoms in most other societies, and certainly not in China. In Ottoman Turkey and Mughal India, there was also an ethnic and religious divide between the ruling élites and merchant groups which were usually dominated by minority groups, such as Armenians and Jews.

The gunpowder empires on land also required a sophisticated infrastructure, in the shape of their artillery parks (cannon and their stores) and the expensive fortress systems states devised for their defence. Whatever the type, military expenditure and activity involved private entrepreneurs and agents to a far greater extent than is implied by the standard discussion of stronger states as the drivers of military capability, action and change.

The potential value of transoceanic-borne expansion to the states of Atlantic Europe did not mean that it crowded out other forms of military activity. Indeed, Spain, France, the Dutch and England all devoted more resources to conflict within Europe than to such expansion. Thus, Philip II of Spain (r. 1556–98) was more concerned with resisting the Ottomans in the Mediterranean and, later, to suppress the Dutch Revolt, than he was expanding his territories in the Americas or Asia. Morocco (rather than South Asia) proved the main field for Portuguese expansion. Indeed, King Sebastian was killed in Morocco on 14 August 1578 in a crippling defeat by a better balanced, disciplined and led army that profited from the use of mounted musketeers. This battle is known as the Battle of the Three Kings or of Wadi-I-Makhazan or of Alcazarquivir, contrasting names that reflect the contrasting role of individual battles in different national histories.

The ships of the period were important not only for their capacity to take troops abroad but also for a ship-killing ability that challenged the role of other navies and permitted an imposition of control over trade. In 1500–38, Portuguese warships off India destroyed the fleets of the Indian states of Calicut and Gujarat, as well as Mameluke and Ottoman squadrons from Egypt, the last two at battles off the important port of Diu in western India in 1509 and 1538 respectively. Such naval superiority was joined to an ability to stage amphibious operations against port cities. Firepower played a role in these, but it would be a mistake to ascribe Portuguese success simply to gunpowder weaponry. Determined action by well-motivated troops was also important. Malacca, a key position on the sea route to China, was captured in 1511.

In Asia, European expansion was at the expense of autonomous cities, relatively weak powers, and areas lacking state structures, for example by Spain in the Philippines from the 1560s. Indeed, despite bold talk of conflict with the major states, notably of an attack on China, none arose, notably because the Europeans were not seeking to create large empires. Moreover, the Asian empires did not see European activities (which were small-scale) as a serious threat. In contrast, the Japanese invasion of Korea in 1592 was intended as a stage in the conquest of China, and this invasion led to a large-scale Chinese intervention on behalf of the Koreans, an intervention that blocked the Japanese, not least by defeating their fleet. This episode was an aspect of the late Ming vitality seen under the Wanli Emperor (r. 1573–1620), during whose reign the Mongol threat to China was also ended.

The European assault on empires was mounted, instead, where the balance of advantage was more favourable than in Asia. In the early-sixteenth century, Spanish adventurers, acting for personal profit as well as the Crown, rapidly destroyed the Aztec Empire of Mesoamerica (central Mexico) as well as the Inca Empire in the Andes (based in modern Peru), the two largest empires in the New World. These victories were traditionally attributed to superior weaponry in the shape of firearms, steel swords and helmets and horses. Other factors, however, also played a major role, including Aztec and Inca leadership and divisions, the extent to which the Spaniards were able to win local allies (including about 150,000 troops against the Aztecs) and the debilitating impact on native societies of disease brought by Europeans, especially smallpox.

Spanish success was consolidated by the ability to incorporate native religions to Christianity in what became a form of syncretic religion. The long-term consequence was that Spain gained a large empire (as Portugal also did in Brazil) without needing to use a substantial force in order to hold it down. At the same time, the Spanish-American Empire yielded resources, both products (especially gold and silver) and control over trade, that provided funds for military activities elsewhere, mostly in Europe. As a result, the movement of bullion from the New World to Spain became a key axis of Spanish power and one to which considerable effort was devoted to protect with naval convoys and the fortification of ports.

Spanish activities arose from a traditional range of European goals, notably dynastic aggrandisement, territorial expansion and religious conflict, with both Muslims and Christians deemed heretics. For many Christian states, the first type of religious conflict centred on warfare with the advancing Ottoman Turks, although there was also conflict with Morocco and with the Muslim khanates in southern Russia. Indeed, the latter conflict was important to the consolidation and far-flung expansion of Russian power, with the most northerly khanate, Kazan, long an obstacle to Russian expansion, conquered by Ivan IV, Ivan the Terrible, in 1552. Astrakhan, further down the River Volga, followed in 1556. In conquering Kazan, firepower, in the shape of Russian cannon, was crucial, but so also was an appropriate strategy as well as the adroit exploitation of divisions among the greatly divided Muslims. These conquests opened the way to further Russian expansion, notably across the Ural Mountains into Siberia, expansion that was to take Russian power to the Pacific by the

1630s. En route, bases were founded at Tobolsk in 1587 and Yakutsk in 1632.

Meanwhile, having conquered the Balkans and Constantinople, the Ottoman Turks pressed on to create an empire that rivalled the Eastern Roman (Byzantine) Empire at its height. If, in 1481, they lost their Italian foothold at Otranto, only limited effort had been devoted to its retention. Far more significantly, the conquest of Syria, Israel, Palestine and Egypt from the Mamelukes in 1516–7 ended intra-Muslim competition in the eastern Mediterranean, provided the prestige gained from guardianship of the Muslim holy places, and gave the Ottomans, under Selim the Grim, control over Egyptian grain supplies and maritime power that they had hitherto lacked. A flank of the Ottoman advance had already been covered when they had become the leading power in the Black Sea region in the fifteenth century.

Yet, the Ottomans could not concentrate on advancing into Christian Europe because they faced to the rear the enmity of the Safavids, the newly established Muslim conquerors of Persia. The Safavids embraced Shiism, a different form of Islam, and challenged the Ottoman position in the Caucasus and eastern Anatolia. The resulting warfare led to Ottoman victory at Chaldiran (1514), a victory that probably owed much to the use of firearms, and, following that, to the Ottoman conquest of what is now Iraq. This warfare, however, also imposed a serious burden on Ottoman warmaking and resources, as well as leading to a lack of focus on expansion into Christian Europe. The latter, nevertheless, saw major advances, especially in the 1520s, when Selim's successor, Suleiman the Magnificent (r. 1520–66), personally led his forces. The Ottomans had made the transition from the traditional Central Asian nomadic force of archers on horseback to a more mixed force including élite infantry equipped with firearms and supported by cannon. The Ottomans, moreover, were precocious in bureaucratic structure and army organization and, as a result, were more capable of deploying large disciplined armies over long distances than Western Europeans at the same time.

Belgrade, which had resisted earlier attack, fell in 1521, and in 1526 Suleiman invaded central Hungary. The Hungarian ruler was defeated and killed at Mohacs in what was a major triumph over Christian heavy cavalry. Suleiman established a client kingdom in the region. However, Vienna was besieged unsuccessfully in 1529, and, in hindsight, that represented a limit to Ottoman expansion, a verdict that was to be endorsed by an ultimately disastrous second siege in 1683.

Yet, in 1529, it was not apparent that the advance had ceased while, over the following 80 years, the Ottomans applied considerable pressure, both on the European mainland, notably in Hungary on the areas that the Habsburgs still controlled, and in the Mediterranean, where Spanish bases in modern Algeria as well as Venetian possessions, particularly Cyprus (1570–1), were captured, although the Ottoman expedition against Malta in 1565 failed. This conflict proved a prime military commitment for much of Christian Europe and serves as a reminder that it is necessary to look at military development in part in terms of the response to outside pressures. There is no more reason why the naval history of sixteenth-century Europe should be written around the English defeat of the Spanish Armada in 1588 (and its subsequent devastation by storms) than the Spanish-Venetian-Papal defeat of the Ottoman fleet at Lepanto off western Greece in 1571, the largest galley battle of the period. This defeat was a heavy blow to the Ottomans, one that reflected a lack of sufficient sailors as well as an over-confidence that fell foul of Venetian firepower. Yet Lepanto, which was intended as a riposte to the Ottoman conquest of Cyprus, did not lead to its recapture, while the Spanish gain of Tunis which followed Lepanto proved only temporary.

The Christian response to the Ottomans involved both military and political dimensions which overlapped, for example with heavy Spanish investment in galleys and in fortifications in the Spanish-ruled kingdom of Naples. The Austrian Habsburgs developed light cavalry able to complement their infantry, but the overall Christian emphasis in the sixteenth and early-seventeenth century was on defence and not attack. The net effect was a focus for, and triumph of, the Catholic Reformation, the strengthening of Catholicism in the sixteenth and early-seventeenth centuries.

In Protestant Europe, this strengthening is best known as the Counter-Reformation, and the emphasis militarily is on the Wars of Religion, notably the Dutch Revolt against rule by Philip II of Spain, a revolt that began in the 1560s. This warfare is then linked to military developments with the discussion of the Dutch role in the early stages of the changes subsequently referred to as the Military Revolution. As with the conflict with the Ottomans, however, this approach risks an excessive militarization of a struggle, the Wars of Religion, which indeed had a military component, but which, as a 'war' in the largest sense, included the battlefields of Church activity, conversion, education, publications, censorship, marriage, the household and poor relief. To use a modern distinction, the conflict was as much about soft power as hard power. It is no accident that the Society of Jesus, or Jesuits, was established by Ignatius Loyola in 1534 as a quasi-military Catholic order. Nor is it surprising that clerics were slaughtered by both sides.

In this respect, the Wars of Religion may look like a prefigurement of the ideological struggles of the twentieth century, for example between Fascism and both liberalism and Communism, or between Communism and liberalism. The Wars of Religion also sat in a tradition of the violent extirpation of heresy seen, for example, in the Crusade against the Albigensians in southern France in the early-thirteenth century and the Hussite wars in Bohemia (Czech Republic) in the early-fifteenth.

Crucial to all ideological conflict, whether in the thirteenth, sixteenth or twentieth centuries, was a degree of popular engagement, a truth that is not captured by the customary emphasis on conventional warfare by regular forces. This problem is even more the case if the emphasis is on the Military Revolution, which, like so many accounts of developments, is top-down. Instead, a narrative of much of the French Wars of Religion from 1562 to 1598, or the Dutch Revolt, or the unsuccessful Northern Rising by Catholics against Elizabeth I of England in 1569, captures a situation in which direct popular action played a prominent role, notably in the form of riots and massacres, while military forces were created by churches and aristocrats able to elicit popular support, which was true, in France and the Low Countries, of both Protestants and Catholics.

This situation remained the case with civil conflict in the early-seventeenth century, for example large-scale peasant uprisings in Austria and France in the 1620 and 1630s, as well as the civil wars in the British Isles in the mid-seventeenth century. In each case, peasant forces were overcome, whereas new armies created in civil wars by the opponents of the sovereign were successful (Scotland and England in mid-seventeenth century), largely successful (Netherlands from the 1570s) or successful for a while (France during the Wars of Religion). This contrast suggests the value of fighting like a regular force. That value was a matter of fighting techniques, but also of experience, leadership and unit cohesion, in part because of the new requirements for drill and synchronization created by the combination of pike and shot. This made it more difficult for untrained (popular) forces to succeed. Moreover, the continuity and legitimation represented by regular forces and governmental forms were particularly important.

The crushing of peasant forces, for example in Gascony in France in 1637, does not attract attention from those who focus on symmetrical warfare, but it was important to the asymmetrical monopolization of organized violence that was a feature of the seventeenth century as governments struggled to contain the tensions created by religious division, economic discontent and social tension. In doing so, governments benefited from the extent to which regular forces were generally supported by the landed élite and thus profited from their local power; when, however, the élite turned to opposition, as in Portugal in 1640 in a successful rejection of rule by the Spanish Habsburgs, then the situation was far more dire. Furthermore, the firearms and discipline of regular forces tended to prevail over the hand-held weapons and inexperience of peasants, especially in a gunpowder environment in which the most successful method was synchronized drill.

This situation looked towards the subsequent pattern across much of the world in which the military played an important part in explicit or implicit support of social control. In this respect, Europe was not different to the non-Western world. Yet, contrasts between the West and the non-West were also readily apparent: in Western Europe it proved impossible to consolidate empires, on the scale of Asia, in part because the Spanish Habsburg attempt to employ the resources of American possessions to implement imperial plans in Europe failed. There was also in Europe a naval emphasis not seen in Asia and Africa, for example with the role of blockade in ending the resistance to the Crown of the Huguenot (French Protestant) strongholds of La Rochelle in 1628, the real end of the French Wars of Religion.

Naval capability enabled the Europeans to create trade routes and imperial systems that spanned much of the world, a situation that was very different to that elsewhere. The projection of this power, however, was not the same as the ability to ensure success. After a major expansion of European power overseas between 1490 and 1560, the situation was less positive thereafter, notably in Morocco, South-West (Angola) and South-East (Mozambique) Africa and in South-East Asia. Yet, in the closing decades of this period, the Europeans established the first bases of what were to be the French and English Empires in North America, with the French in the St Lawrence valley where Québec was founded in 1608, and the English in Virginia (1607) and Massachusetts (1620). Conflict with the native peoples played a role in this process, particularly in Virginia in the 1620s and in the English victory over the Pequots in Connecticut the following decade.

If the weapons used by Western forces outside Europe were similar to those on the battlefields of the Thirty Years' War in Europe

(1618–48), the scale and nature of conflict were different, although there were similarities to the 'small warfare' of skirmishing seen in Europe. There were also similarities to the animosity across ethnic and/or religious lines seen in some European conflicts, such as Ireland, where English forces established control as a result of bitter warfare in 1595–1603 and 1649–52. The net effect of conflict by Western forces outside Europe was an extension of European power that was of great significance for the future politics of the world.

The distinguished military historian of eighteenth-century Europe, Christopher Duffy, remarked that the 'notion of a "Military Revolution"' has distorted the study of early-modern military history for decades from the 1950s. This blunt comment contrasts markedly with the views of those who still find the thesis useful, indeed fundamental. Geoffrey Parker, the key figure, is preparing, with relatively few changes, a third edition of his seminal book on the Military Revolution 1500–1800, a work first published in 1988. Where does this leave readers, for the thesis itself is of importance not simply as a means of shaping our understanding of early modern European, indeed, world military history, and the period as a whole, but also as a key instance of the process of military revolution in history, a fundamental concept for the subject?

The idea of an early-modern European military revolution was not invented by Michael Roberts, but, in his inaugural lecture of 1955, he gave it shape and prominence. Focusing on the period 1560–1660, but as part of a longer-term process in military change, stemming from the introduction of portable firearms, Roberts drew connections between military technology and techniques, and larger historical consequences. He specifically argued that innovations in tactics, drill and doctrine by the Dutch and Swedes, designed to maximize the benefit of firearms, led to a need for more trained troops and thus for more permanent state military forces. Parker was to claim that the introduction of volley fire in the Dutch army in the 1590s was to transform Western warfare, ensuring that firepower, not manpower, would decide the outcome of battles.

The Roberts' thesis of the Military Revolution was also transformed by Parker in a number of fruitful directions, not least with an emphasis on fortification techniques known as the *trace italienne* which responded to the possibilities and challenge of artillery; on the Spanish army, a key force in the late-sixteenth century; on naval developments, specifically the capability provided by gunned warships; and on the global dimensions of the Revolution. As a result, Parker linked European military changes to the Rise of the West, a central issue in world history. The question of the role of military revolutions in history is of even greater consequence, because of the role of the supposed Revolution in Military Affairs in recent and contemporary American military thought, doctrine, planning and procurement.

The global perspective Parker encouraged certainly remains valuable. Yet, the concept of an early-modern military revolution has proved far less helpful for 1650–1800, the second half of the period designated by Parker. This point is true both for conflict within Europe and for that further afield. Indeed, Parker's argument that changes in European warmaking, specifically the development of the 'artillery fortress', led to a fundamental shift in the military balance between the West and the non-West, is of only limited applicability for East Asia or Africa in the period 1650–1830. The failures, in the late-seventeenth century, of the Dutch in Taiwan, of Russia in the Amur Valley and of Portugal on the Swahili Coast and in Zimbabwe are all notable; and this is not an exhaustive list of European military failure. Even in North America, English and French colonists repeatedly found their expansion of the frontier contested and limited by native Americans.

There are of course European military successes that could also be noted, particularly those of the Austrians in 1683–97 and 1716–8 in driving the Ottoman Turks from Vienna and then in reconquering Hungary for Christendom, and conquering it, for the first time, for the Habsburgs, ensuring that their empire increasingly had a strong Eastern European, rather than German, dimension. Moreover, it was scarcely the case that non-Western forces were attacking Western Europe. Indeed, the latter idea was satirized by Henry Fielding in his play *The Coffee-House Politician* (1730) in the shape of Politic's fears about an Ottoman invasion of England. The idea was also mentioned by the historian Edward Gibbon as an event that would represent a fundamental change to current circumstances. Nevertheless, compared to the scale of Western expansion in 1850–1920, that in 1650–1780 was modest, although steady Russian pressure south at the expense of the Ottomans was significant, and led to territorial gains at the end of wars in 1739 and 1774. Rather than assuming any European superiority, whether based on (or amounting to) military revolution or not, it is more appropriate to note the more complex, contingent and varied nature of relative military capability; and also to give due weight to the non-military factors for differential regional success.

Moreover, research on warfare within Europe has emphasized the extent to which the model of organization and tactics that proved the focus of attention for Roberts and, with significant variations, Parker should be treated, not as the definitive European model, but, rather, as the most influential of several models. In particular, attention has been directed to an important contrasting model in Eastern Europe, with a heavier stress on cavalry. This and other contrasts underline the extent to which there was no one obvious best practice, which can be identified with a Military Revolution, and the diffusion of which can and should be studied.

Instead, there was a complex process of interaction within and between military environments. In this interaction, best practice should be understood in terms of the specific requirements of particular environments, rather than of the possibilities presented by one weapons system composed of a particular weapon and certain formations and tactics. This point can be taken further because study of the 'face' of battle, the individual and collective realities of conflict, suggests that cohesion, morale, impact and persistence in hand-to-hand fighting could be much more important in both characterizing this 'face of battle' and in ensuring success than tactical sophistication in the shape of deployment, unit size and firepower drill.

Paradoxically, uniformity in fighting method became more apparent in Europe from the eighteenth century, with infantry armed with flintlock muskets equipped with bayonets. The fearsome edges and points of bayonets altered warfare by transforming the foot soldiers' capability in combat. The early plug bayonet, introduced in the early 1640s, was inserted in the musket barrel and therefore prevented firing leading to problems for William III's suporters when attacked by Scottish Highlanders at Killiecrankie in 1689. This bayonet was based on weapons used by hunters and was named after the town of Bayonne in south-west France. The hunters' weapons were daggers that, if necessary, could be inserted into muskets, making them a useful weapon against boars, which serves as a reminder of the overlap between hunting and conflict. It has been claimed that the French army was using the bayonet by 1642. Use rapidly spread, and by the 1670s specialized units such as dragoons and fusiliers were being issued with bayonets. At the siege of Spanish-held Valenciennes in 1677, the first French bayonet attack occurred. By the 1680s, bayonets were far more common. They were essentially, by now, double-edged dagger blades that were about 12 inches long attached to a handle that was about 12 inches long. This was designed to be the same diameter as the musket's bore. The handle was fixed in position by working it into the musket.

The plug bayonet was replaced by ring-and-socket bayonets, developed in the 1680s, which allowed firing with the blade in place. The bayonet was turned and locked in place, ensuring firmness in combat. This enhanced capability led to the phasing out of the now redundant pike, which enhanced overall firepower and resulted in longer and thinner linear formations of infantry all armed with muskets equipped with bayonets. This, more effective, weaponry resulted in the end of body armour (pikemen wore breastplates), a step that increased the mobility of troops. Ironically, however, the shift to the bayonet was not the focus of the classic Military

Revolution of Roberts and Parker, both of whom concentrated on the period prior to 1660, when variety in weaponry had been more apparent.

An emphasis on specific European (and non-European) military environments in part serves to highlight the conceptual issue of the role of tasking or goals in helping determine the development of particular armies and navies. For example, post-war downsizings of armies and navies in the seventeenth and eighteenth centuries indicated that, as today, force structures were adapted to purpose. This adaptation was an aspect of the dynamic interaction of strategic cultures with the very volatile international relations of the period, each involving the particular dynastic strategies or individual drives of rulers. The emphasis here is on variety – that the navy of Oman or France had a different task than that of Britain – and therefore on the danger of assuming an obvious best practice that acted as a paradigm or model with which other powers sought to conform, the method used by those discussing the putative Military Revolution and other standard narratives of military change.

Thus, the argument here is that the concept of an early-modern military revolution has become a catchall – widely employed but lacking in precision, and also that the concept has been used with an attention to process that is (necessarily) patchy and is inclined to emphasize the diffusion of the supposed master models of combat and organization, rather than the extent to which borrowings were adapted to existing military systems. Moreover, the concept of such a revolution rests on a 'push' theory of warfare, which interprets military developments in terms of the material culture of war, specifically the weaponry. This approach devotes far too little attention to 'pull' factors, in terms of the purposes of military capability, the use of the military, and related force structures, and doctrines. There is scant sign of a fully-fledged revolution in these purposes or 'taskings' on land in the early-modern period, the term employed to describe the sixteenth to eighteenth centuries; although at sea there was a new interest in protecting long-range maritime links.

Military realities were both too complex (geographically) and too dependent on previous experiences (political, cultural and economic) to make the term Military Revolution useful as a phrase to describe or encapsulate the military changes of the period. There were changes, in technologies, organizations and attitudes, but they were neither revolutionary nor universal. Instead, the correct emphasis, as so often in military history, is on continuities, not least in terms both of reasons for conflict and of limitations, especially in tactical, operational and strategic military effectiveness, administrative structures and support, relative capability with regard to non-European military systems and European transoceanic impact on land.

To stress continuity entails noting similarities in warfare. For example, mid-seventeenth century battles witnessed a greater role for firepower than those of the late-fifteenth century, but sieges remained a mixture of bombardment, blockade and storming, while the role of cavalry and light forces in raiding territory and denying opponents the opportunity to raise supplies was still crucial in operational terms. Cavalry also continued to play a major role in battles (unlike the situation by the 1860s), contributing to their character as combined arms actions, and thus to the need for commanders able to co-ordinate forces successfully. The ability to rally cavalry that had defeated opposing cavalry and to redirect it against infantry was important in French victory over the Spaniards at Rocroi in 1643 and that of the English Parliamentarians over the Royalists at Naseby in 1645 in the English Civil War. Indeed, it has been argued that cavalry was really the decisive (battlefield) arm for much seventeenth-century warfare, including the English Civil War.

On land, the supposed Military Revolution is bound up with debate about the intentions of rulers, the nature of early-modern states, and the degree of continuity with medieval states and warmaking. There is a misleading tendency in work by some early-modernists to treat medieval warfare as primitive in comparison with what was to come, and also to present it in teleological terms, with an emphasis on the development of infantry and on archers as progenitors of the subsequent introduction of hand-held gunpowder weaponry. This approach has led to a slighting of the variety of medieval warfare and to a misleading account of its development. The reduction of medieval development to a simple formula, 'first it was knights and castles, and then infantry and guns', is particularly unfortunate. A consideration of the medieval background also underlines the need to assess the potential for technological transformation then, and at other times, in its social and political contexts.

It can be argued that medieval precedents constitute a prehistory of the Military Revolution, but this can be reconceptualized to suggest that the so-called Revolution, far from being revolutionary, was in fact another stage in the process by which European medieval warfare developed. In particular, medieval warfare displayed a considerable ability to innovate, not only in tactics and fortifications, but also in the infrastructure of military preparedness. Moreover, although gunpowder provided the basis for different forms of hand-held projectile weaponry and artillery, the technique of massed projectile weaponry was not new. The general disparagement of the medieval experience has led to an over-valuation of early-modern changes.

It is also appropriate to draw attention to the deficiencies of firearms in the sixteenth to eighteenth centuries. The accuracy of smoothbore guns was limited while spherical bullets were less aerodynamically effective than their nineteenth-century replacements. Recharging and reloading from the muzzle (end) of the gun (rather than, as later, the breech) increased the time taken to fire, and the long reloading cycle led to acute vulnerability for the musketeers, especially to attack from cavalry. Troops were deployed near their opponents because the ability of spherical shot to inflict lethal wounds at other than short range was limited, and was further decreased by the impact on muzzle velocity of the large windage (gap between projectile and inside of barrel) made necessary by the difficulty of casting accurate shot.

A functional account of variety in military practice in Europe, and indeed further afield, can be taken further to consider the diverse meanings of the culture of war, a field of discussion in military history that has excited considerable interest in recent years. The idea of distinctive national cultures of war queries anew the notion of a uniform best practice, and thus moves attention to an understanding of developments as necessarily varied in goal, content and chronology. The result may appear to offer a rather bitty and inconsequential account of the period, in place of the grand sweep of clear-cut and general developments in warmaking, but this approach accurately reflects the absence of such a sweep.

Related to this, the discussion so far on the early-modern period has concentrated on top-down perspectives, particularly war and the rise of the modern state, the transformation of state systems, resource mobilization, the notion of paradigm militaries and macro- or overall perspectives on decisiveness and victory. There is room, instead, for more micro-perspectives, encouraged by the current, more cultural approach, for example discussion of the experience of war. These perspectives may offer new insights on established questions such as the extent to which war was total, at least as understood by contemporaries.

The brutality of both conflict and the treatment of civilians emerges repeatedly in accounts of early-modern warfare. In part, the latter reflected the need to seize supplies, but there was also a habitual brutalization not least as far as civilians of different ethnicities and religions were concerned. Nevertheless, it is unclear that early-modern warfare was more brutal, in Europe or elsewhere, than its medieval predecessor. One aspect of brutality was the enslavement of the defeated, the basis of the slave trade from Africa to the Americas that developed in the sixteenth century and became large-scale the following century. Yet, such enslavement was scarcely new, and there was already an active slave trade within Africa and from Africa to the Middle East.

Presentism is always a problem, but it is worth asking how far the understanding of conflict in Iraq, Afghanistan and elsewhere, from

2003, may have affected the analysis of early-modern warfare. These conflicts certainly underline the ambiguous character of victory, the extent to which success in battle is not automatically the same as triumph in war, and the problems that high-specification weaponry and militaries may face in confronting insurgencies. Reading back, these conflicts also underline the extent to which earlier Western successes depended, at least in part, on the co-operation or at least consent of non-Western forces and peoples, as with the Spanish conquest under Hernán Cortés of the Aztecs in Mexico in 1519–21, a triumph that owed much to local co-operation against Aztec hegemony.

Such an emphasis on consent does not deny a role for Western force multipliers, such as firepower and artillery fortresses, but it does suggest that they need to be put in a context of the requirement in many cases of anchoring success in consent. This situation was also true for non-Western invaders, such as the Mughals in northern India in the sixteenth century: the Mughals benefited, in particular, from winning the support of the Rajputs. Consent could take varied forms, including religious syncretism, as with the spread of Christianity in Latin America, and also service in the military of the imperial power.

There has been revived interest in recent years in the concept of military revolution, as work on the supposed contemporary Revolution in Military Affairs (RMA) has led to consideration of reputed antecedents or, looked at differently, to the discovery of a supporting history that can lend credence to the idea of an RMA. This discovery is a somewhat dubious process, not least because the self-conscious character of the RMA was not matched to the same extent in the early-modern period, particularly because there was also then a strong, continued and, in many respects, new belief in the value of Classical exemplars, and therefore a looking back to the ancient, especially Roman but also Greek and Macedonian, world, and to its military iconography, formations, tactics, weaponry and authors, for example Vegetius. This 'return to the past' served to validate new emphases. Whether or not there is an effective modern RMA, as opposed to a discourse to that end, that offers no proof of a similar situation in the early-modern period.

Moreover, the conflicts of recent years have underlined the varied character of modern warfare. This variety has implications for what is understood as modernization, and for what seems relevant in this account. The contrasting view of two decades ago was of modernization in terms of the move towards the total war capability and doctrine then held to define modern warfare, especially with the maximization of destructiveness through the enhancement of firepower. Now, instead, there is scepticism about glib uses of the concepts of total and modern warfare, and also greater interest in limited warfare, which indeed makes aspects of the doctrine and practice of *ancien régime* (European 1660–1789) conflict appear relevant. What John Lynn has termed the 'war-as-process' of the early-modern period was more like war since 1945 than is the swift decisiveness of Napoleonic war-as-event, although the latter was similar to, for example, the swift Israeli triumph in the Six Days' War of 1967.

Michael Roberts argued that innovations between 1560–1660 in tactics, drill and doctrine by the Dutch and Swedes, designed to maximize the benefit of firearms, led to a need for more trained troops and thus for permanent forces, with major political and social consequences, not least a level of administrative support, in the supply of money, men and provisions, that produced new financial demands and governmental institutions. Thus, the modern art of war made possible and necessary the creation of the modern state. This is an attractive theory, but the recent reconceptualization of the 'absolutist' state of early-modern Europe has, instead, put an emphasis on co-operation between élites and rulers, rather than on the coercive power of the latter, supposedly gained by developments in military capability and organization: all those royal cannon bringing down baronial walls. The idea that rulers were able to direct societies no longer seems convincing.

Instead, a reconciliation of rulers and élites, in the second half of the seventeenth century, after the civil wars of the mid-seventeenth century, provided the basis for a process of domestic consolidation, the *ancien régime*, and for, at least attempted, external expansion by a number of states, including Austria, England, China, France, Mughal India, Russia and the Ottoman Empire. Military service entailed the nobility accepting obedience and subordination, while the monarchy was able to co-opt the resources of the aristocracy to support the army; but this was a matter of reconciliation rather than coercion. In terms of stability, this reconciliation was most effective when aristocratic élites were integrated not only into armies but also into bureaucracies, as this gave a peace-time coherence that was otherwise lacking if warfare was the means of unity.

If change in the social politics and political consequences of force in early-modern Europe can now be presented in more gradualist, and less revolutionary, terms, than would have been the case two decades ago, then this matches the apparent long-term character of technological, scientific and intellectual developments. Once a chronological focus is added, then 'long-term' can also appear to mean slow, notably in contrast with the usual assumptions that revolutions mean rapidity. However, slowness should not be seen as a criticism, not least because change was difficult and, indeed, often a problem to overcome, while the character of military life and capability were frequently intractable.

Furthermore, in place of a 'big bang' process of development, often seen in the language of military revolutions, or of a triumphalist account of change towards clear improvement, comes the understanding that incremental change poses its own problems of assessing best practice, as well as the difficulties of determining whether it was appropriate to introduce new methods. Indeed the habitual use by writers of models of diffusion, and of the language of adaptation, makes change in the past appear far less problematic than was the case.

The same is true of the use of the concept and phraseology of revolution. This problem with the assumptions expressed in and flowing from the use of language is the case not simply of the early-modern Military Revolution but also of the idea of revolutionary change in 1775–1815 with American Revolutionary (1775–83), French Revolutionary (1792–9) and Napoleonic (1799–1815) warfare. The latter argument for revolutionary change in fact underplays the extent to which there was continuity between *ancien régime* conflict and that in 1775–1815, just as there may have been more continuity between the fifteenth and sixteenth centuries than those who focus on the early-modern Military Revolution sometimes allow for. Moreover, the notion that French Revolutionary and Napoleonic conflict transformed warfare and brought forward modernity again underplays the variety of modern warfare, not least in scale, goal and intensity. If modern warfare is not necessarily total, total warfare is not necessarily modern and can therefore be separated from any developmental model of conflict.

The argument in this chapter might seem to imply that there were no revolutionary changes that transformed the nature of warfare, but this is not the case. Developments in weaponry, force structures, doctrine and planning could indeed be sufficiently radical, rapid and of great consequence to be referred to as revolutionary, as with the impact of submarines and air power on naval conflict in the Second World War. What is less clear is that the developments in the period 1400–1820 conformed to this revolutionary type. Yet, obviously there were changes on land and at sea, not least the key organizational one of the rise of large permanent professional state-directed armies and navies in Europe, while, on the global level, the expansion of European power at sea and overseas was very significant. This expansion increasingly influenced much of the world power system, although, as yet, Western expansion was far from comprehensive in its impact, a point discussed at the beginning of the following chapter.

The application of new knowledge was also apparent, and seems to have been particularly important in Europe, not least because printing led there to an active book world in which new ideas were rapidly disseminated, a contrast with the more restricted nature of printing in, for example, the Ottoman Empire. Thus, in 1606, Galileo published *Operations of the Geometric and Military Compass*, a work in which he discussed such problems as how best to calibrate guns for cannonballs of different materials and weight, and also how to deploy armies with unequal fronts and flanks. In many respects, one strand of military development represented the interaction of the new, heavily mathematical Scientific Revolution, and the opportunities it provided for analysis and presentation of ballistics, fortification and drill, with, on the other hand, the interests of governments in enhancing their capability. This strand became more pronounced in the second half of the seventeenth century, with works such as Allain Manesson-Mallet's *Les Travaux de Mars, ou la fortification nouvelle tant régulière, qu'irrégulière* (Paris, 1672). War became part of the knowledge economy and system. The availability of printed treatises and manuals contributed to a literature on drill that matched a conviction of its value and a regimentation of knowledge.

At the same time, there were significant continuities in capability and warmaking, for example the dependence for movement on human and animal calories or the wind, the restricted speed of command and control practices, the need to mass troops for both shock and firepower and, more generally, the powerful resource constraints of primarily relatively low-production agrarian eco-nomies. Even as late as the First World War (1914–18), while railways were very important, troops walked to war from the railhead and depended heavily on animals to transport materials, as they had done for centuries, indeed millennia. This list of continuities, which can be extended, makes discussion in terms of military revolution highly problematic, but the debate will continue.

From the Mid-Seventeenth Century Crisis to the Age of Revolutions, 1630–1800

It is ironic that warfare in Europe dominates the attention of military historians during the lifetime of Louis XIV of France, the Sun King, 1643–1715, as however fascinating his ambitions and the clash between France and Habsburgs, this was not a period in which that warfare, and indeed developments in conflict there, can be readily linked to Europe's relative capability on a world scale. More significantly, this was not an age in which the European powers greatly increased their overseas sway. Like all comments, this one can be qualified and refined, and has been by means of discussing the period in terms of the European Military Revolution considered in the previous chapter; but the argument here for (relative) European limitations is supported by a careful consideration of the contemporary comparative dimension, as well as the additional one offered by comparison with the greater strides made over the following 72 years (1716–88). The latter was a period in which there were significant European gains in India, South-East Europe and North America, as well as expansion in South America, and, at the end, the establishment of a British settlement in Australia.

An awareness of the limited extent of European expansion in the period 1643–1715, a limited extent that may owe much to war within Christendom including those due to Louis XIV, can be dramatized by reference to failures and setbacks. They stand as an important qualification of the impression created by the serious Ottoman (Turkish) defeat outside Vienna in 1683, which brought to a dramatic end the last Ottoman advance into central Europe and was followed, by 1699, by the Austrian conquest of most of Hungary. Prominent among these failures were those of the Dutch in Taiwan, the French in Siam (Thailand), the English in Tangier, the Russians in the Amur Valley and against the Crimean Tatars, both in the 1680s, and the Portuguese in Mombassa. The list of failures culminates with two defeats at the hands of the Ottomans, those of Peter the Great of Russia on the River Pruth when he invaded the Balkans in 1711, seriously underestimating Ottoman strength, and of the Venetians in the Morea (Peloponnese) in 1715: the Ottomans then held this part of Greece until the late 1820s. Looking beyond Louis' reign, other important failures included that of the Austrians at the hands of the Ottomans in 1739, with failure in the field followed by the cession of Belgrade.

The context for these failures is usually given as that of European history, European power and the trajectory of the rise of the West. Thus, defeats are smoothed out in terms of a longer-term success, which is a view that has some merit. Yet a more pertinent context is provided by that of the dynamism and variety of military capability and warfare across the world, with the Europeans influenced by, as well as influencing, other powers. In order to understand this process, it is necessary to see these other powers not as lesser forces that were bound to fail, in, for example, some chronologically receding aspect of the Eastern Question (the fate of the then weak Ottoman Empire in the late-nineteenth century), but, instead, as powers that did not operate, and were not considered, in terms of obvious and inevitable failure.

If this is true for powers that competed with Western states, it was even more the case for those for whom such competition was non-existent, for example Japan. Moreover, even if the former category of powers is considered, it is mistaken to imagine that confrontation and conflict with the West came first. This situation is true, for example, for China, which was nowhere near as concerned by war with Russia nor the control of Taiwan as a Western-centric account might suggest. For China, the key issues and challenges were those with other Asian powers, first the Manchus in the early-seventeenth century and later, from the 1680s to the 1750s, the Dzhungars.

In turn, Persia lost Baku and provinces on the western and southern side of the Caspian Sea to attack by Peter the Great of Russia in 1722–3; but the overthrow of the Safavid dynasty (which had ruled Persia since the 1500s) by Afghan attack in 1723 was far more serious, although the Afghans were unable to sustain their control. In the face of disease and Persian pressure, the Russians were unable to hold onto their gains on the southern side of the Caspian and they abandoned them in 1732. Even the Ottomans remained as worried about Persia, with whom there was a serious struggle from the 1720s to the 1740s, repeating that of a century earlier, as about the European powers. The Persians, their power revived under Nader Shah, could threaten such key Ottoman cities as Baghdad and Mosul, which were unsuccessfully attacked in 1732–3 and 1743, and 1743 respectively. In contrast, Russian gains, such as Azov to the north-east of the Black Sea in 1696, were peripheral, and, initially in the case of Azov, temporary.

Thus, there is no central theme or narrative for global military history in terms of the responses to Western power. Instead, and this is the key point, it is necessary to work with the absence of such a central theme or narrative in order to understand the period. This argument can be taken further by noting the problems with any idea of substitute themes for those of the Military Revolution (see last chapter) or the rise of the West, for example the theme of the recovery of Eurasian states after the mid-seventeenth-century crisis leading to greater military strength. However plausible, such themes face serious problems in terms of the viability of overall models.

In this chapter therefore, there is no special approach that will provide clear shape for the subject. Yet, in emphasizing the protean character of war and the military, it is necessary to provide a sense of more than one thing after the other. The emphasis, certainly for conflict on land, should be on East Asia, as China, the world's most populous state, found its fortunes transformed by war in this period. Nothing in the European world compared to the scale and drama of the overthrow of Ming China, nor to the size of the forces involved.

The overlap with Louis XIV's reign, and indeed with the Frondes, or rebellions, in France of 1648–53, was coincidental but provides a good point of comparison. Under frequent attack from the Manchus to the north, Ming China succumbed to rebellion from within, as Habsburg Austria had not done in the 1620s, while Habsburg Spain similarly survived the 1640s, and, despite the Frondes, no comparable threat was aimed against Bourbon France. In China, Li Zicheng, a rebel who had become a powerful regional warlord, benefited from the extent to which Ming forces and fortifications were concentrated on defending northern China from Manchu attack from the steppe, and not on confronting rebellion. In 1644, he advanced on Beijing. The garrison marched out but proved unequal to the task, and, as the capital fell, the incompetent Chongzhen Emperor committed suicide, bringing to an end a dynasty that had begun in 1368. Li proclaimed the Shun dynasty, but his army was poorly disciplined and he lacked the supports of legitimacy, powerful allies and administrative apparatus. Here there is a powerful comparison with elements of European politics.

The fall of the Ming dynasty was a key reminder of the political context of conflict. So also was the aftermath. Wu Sangui, who commanded the largest Chinese army on the northern frontier, opposing the Manchus, refused to submit to Li and, instead, turned to the Manchus. They felt that the death of the Ming Emperor provided them with greater opportunity and legitimacy for their attempt to take over China. In the Battle of Shanhaiguan (the Battle of the Pass), on 27 May 1644, a key clash which rarely features in the lists of decisive battles in world history, the joint Manchu-Ming army defeated Li, with the ability of the Manchu cavalry to turn Li's flank proving decisive. Wu pursued the fleeing Li and was responsible for his death in 1645.

In turn, Chinese units were reorganized by the Manchus, who recruited some of the leading Ming generals and used them to help in the conquest of central and southern China, which fell more speedily than when the Mongols had invaded China in the thirteenth century (although they were to fall far more rapidly to the Chinese Communists in 1949). Again, the key clash for mid-seventeenth-century China was scarcely with the West. Moreover, Western forces did not play any role in the struggles within China, a marked contrast with the situation during the Taipeng Rebellion of the mid-nineteenth century.

These Manchu campaigns, the first conquest of China by non-Chinese forces since the Mongol invasions of the thirteenth century, indicate the need for care in reading from models of military capability and progress based on Western Europe. More particularly, the literature on state development and military revolution presumes a synergy in which governmental sophistication and needs play a key role in military capability and indeed provide definitions for progress and success. Instead, the overthrow of the Ming underlines the extent to which administrative continuity and sophistication, which the Ming certainly possessed, did not suffice for victory. More generally, it is overly easy to read back from later circumstances and to fail to note the extent to which, in the early-modern period, the degree of organization required to create and support a large permanent long-range navy, or large permanent armies, was not required to maintain military forces fit for purpose across most of the world, nor to ensure success.

Similarly, it is mistaken to read back from the modern perception of the effectiveness of infantry and artillery firepower, and of the attendant relationship between disciplined, well-drilled and well-armed permanent firepower forces, and those that were not so armed. In practice, cavalry remained key to much conflict in seventeenth-century China and India, and also continued to be important in Europe. On the world scale, the principal limit on cavalry was that of disease and climate, which greatly restricted the use of horses in Africa. There were no horses in Australia. In America, horses (like guns) had rapidly ceased to be a monopoly of the European invaders. The diffusion of horses and guns to the Native Americans led to changes in warmaking by the latter, changes that were operational as well as tactical.

If military 'progress' is difficult to define, the same is true of political 'progress'. As with the 'decline and fall' of imperial Rome, and yet also the role of 'barbarians', both in defeating Rome and in fighting for it, there were not clear-cut sides in seventeenth-century China, and the 'overthrow' that is to be explained is not as readily apparent as it might appear. Instead, the Manchu conquest involved redefinitions of cultural loyalty in which distinctions between Chinese and 'barbarian' became less apparent and definitions less rigid. Indeed, the Manchu state owned its success to its syncretic character, which highlighted the extent to which such a means, while crucial for European success in the aptly named Latin America, did not generally operate similarly for the Europeans in North America, Africa or the Balkans.

These problems of definition, both military and political, were even more apparent when the Manchus encountered strong resistance in southern China, where they were challenged by Zheng Chenggong (known to Europeans as Coxinga). He was a figure who can be domesticated for European readers by comparative reference to the Austrian entrepreneur-general Wallenstein (1583–1634), a key figure in Europe prior to the Peace of Westphalia of 1648 with its lack of a monopolization of force by sovereign rulers, and indeed of a clear differentiation of the latter from others wielding power, such as mercenaries. With the profits of piracy and trade, Zheng, a warlord of note, developed a large fleet based in Fujian in south-east China and amassed a substantial army of over 50,000 men, some of whom were equipped with European-style weapons. In 1656–8, Zheng regained much of southern China for the Ming. The large force he led to the siege of Nanjing in 1659 was mostly armed with swords: two-handed long heavy swords, or short swords carried with shields. In a clear contrast with European warfare, the soldiers wore mail coats to protect themselves against bullets. Zheng's army included cannon and musketeers, but also an archery corps that was more effective than his musketeers. This army was defeated outside Nanjing by Manchu cavalry and infantry attacks. After the Manchus advanced into Fujian in 1659, Zheng turned his attention to Taiwan, where he landed in 1661. The Dutch base, Fort Zeelandia, capitulated to him the following February. Dutch attempts to re-establish their position were all unsuccessful, whereas a Manchu expedition gained Taiwan from Zheng's successor in 1683. It is too easy to contrast the two, as the Dutch efforts were in fact mounted from Batavia (Djakarta), their base in the East Indies, which is much further away. Nevertheless, there is an instructive contrast between the Dutch failure and the later British ability, by the Treaty of Nanjing of 1842, to force the Chinese to accept their capture of Hong Kong in the First Opium War.

Having conquered southern China, the Manchus were, in turn, challenged by the ultimately unsuccessful Sanfen Rebellion of 1673–81, a rebellion that highlighted the issue of control over the military. This issue was not a key matter in Europe in the late-seventeenth century as generals and armies did not tend to rebel, although John Churchill, later 1st Duke of Marlborough, abandoned James II in 1688 when William of Orange, William III, invaded England. However, the issue of control was important to Russian politics in the 1680 and 1690s, and Peter the Great had to suppress the *Streltsy* regiments who rebelled in 1698. His suppression of this rebellion proved a key step in his modernization of the Russian army on what was becoming the standard European pattern. The *Streltsy* Rebellion, however, was a matter of garrison mutinies and not regional-based opposition such as the Sanfen Rebellion in China.

In China, this rebellion, also called the War of the Three Feudatories, was begun by powerful generals who were provincial governors, especially Wu Sangui who controlled most of south-western China. The Feudatories overran most of south China, but were driven back to the south-west by 1677 thanks to the Manchus' use of Green Standard Troops: loyal Chinese forces. Earlier, Manchu units had failed to defeat the rebels, and this failure, and the corresponding success of the Green Standard Troops, helped in the consolidation of a new political system in which Manchu tribesmen could no longer challenge the ruler's adoption of Chinese administrative techniques, personnel and priorities. The banner system enabled Chinese, Manchus and Mongols to operate together as part of a single military machine, and this machine was to last longer than that created by the Mongols in the thirteenth century. This integration was related to that of infantry and cavalry units. The war itself saw a large-scale use of firearms on both sides, as well as of elephants by the rebels.

The success of the dynamic Kangxi Emperor (r. 1662–1723) in overcoming rebellion was matched by that in defeating a challenge from the steppe. It is difficult to know how far Chinese victory over the Dzhungars should be explained in systemic terms, possibly with reference to the strength of the Manchu–Ming synergy, and how far in terms of more specific factors, not least the contingencies of campaigning, but the verdict, nevertheless, was instructive. The western Mongolian tribes, known collectively as the Oirats, had united in the dynamic new Dzhungar Confederation from 1635 and had made major gains under Taishi Galdan Boshughtu (r. 1671–97). In 1687, the Dzhungars advanced into eastern Mongolia, bringing them close to confrontation with China. In 1690, the two armies clashed at Ulan Butong, 300 kilometres north of Beijing. In a reminder of tactical variety on the world scale, Galdan's defensive tactics, not least sheltering his men behind camels armoured with felt, limited the effectiveness of the Chinese artillery but the Chinese drove their opponents from the field, although they were unable to mount an effective pursuit due to a shortage of food and because their horses were exhausted. The Chinese commander was happy to negotiate a truce.

In 1696, however, the Kangxi Emperor advanced north across the Gobi Desert, although this test of the logistical resources of the Chinese army led his advisers to urge him to turn back before it starved. Galdan's army, however, was destroyed at the Battle of Jao Modo, thanks in part to the Kangxi Emperor being backed by Galdan's rebellious nephew, Tsewang Rabdan. Again, a contrast with warfare in Europe was notable, although European forces operating both there and further afield, such as Charles XII of Sweden when he moved into Ukraine in 1708–9, sought to exploit such rivalries. After another effective Chinese campaign in the winter of 1696–7, Galdan died in suspicious circumstances. The Manchu system had delivered a decisive verdict despite the difficulty of the terrain, the distance from Chinese sources of supply, and the long months of campaigning. The combination of effective forces with successful logistical and organizational systems made the Manchu army arguably the most impressive in the world, although there was nothing to match the impressive fortification and siege capabilities developed for Louis XIV by Sébastien Le Prestre de Vauban, who was appointed Commissioner General of Fortifications in 1678.

By the 1690s, not only were the Europeans proving more successful against the Ottomans on land than hitherto, but China had its strongest and most advanced northern frontier for centuries. The combination of Chinese and steppe forces and systems ensured that the problems that had beset Ming China had been overcome. The strength of Manchu China owed much to the resulting advance, as the lands that had formed the initial Manchu homeland as well as the Manchu acquisitions in eastern Mongolia in the 1690s had been the source of intractable problems for the Ming. The frontier had been overcome, or rather pushed back, a process underlined when settlement was supported in conquered areas in order to provide resources to sustain the army, and to deny them to any possible opponent, a longstanding process in Chinese history.

Comparisons and contrasts can be extended by considering India. The Mughals, although they had major achievements, not least in conquering the Deccan sultanates of Golconda (near Hyderabad) and Bijapur in 1685–7, were unable to maintain their position against rebellion, and in particular proving unsuccessful in suppressing the Marathas of the western Deccan. Yet, before the emphasis is put on failure, it is worth noting that this impression owed more to subsequent developments, with the Mughal Emperors of the early-eighteenth century unable to sustain gains or to prevent the empire from suffering rapid collapse. In the shorter term, the Emperor Aurangzeb (r. 1658–1707) had succeeded in gaining a degree of hegemony within India that neither the Habsburg rulers of Spain and Austria nor Louis XIV of France could match in Europe. Yet, from another perspective, the competitive military emulation that this 'multipolarity' caused in Christendom resulted in an increase in the aggregate (total) effectiveness of the Christian European powers, and also kept their forces combat-worthy.

Louis XIV briefly, in the 1680s and early-1690s, had the largest navy in the world, part of a pattern of European predominance with his position coming between those of the Dutch and English/ British navies as world leaders. The contrast here with the situation outside Europe where there were not comparable naval powers was readily apparent, although non-European powers could still take a role at sea. Indeed, the Ottoman fleet helped in the capture of the Mediterranean island of Crete from Venice in 1645–69. Further east, large squadrons of Mughal riverboats, carrying cannon, played a major role in defeating the Arakan fleet in 1666, although the expansion of Mughal power against Arakan also owed much to operations on land, especially road building.

The Omani Arabs were especially impressive. They captured the Portuguese base of Muscat in 1650, part of a process by which Portuguese power in the Indian Ocean was under serious pressure from local powers as well as the Dutch. On the basis of the ships the Omanis seized, and the hybrid culture they took over, they created a formidable navy with well-gunned warships. It was the largest fleet in the western part of the Indian Ocean, and thus a key element in its trade. Benefiting from the use of European mariners, and from the assistance of Dutch and English navigators, gunners and arms suppliers, the Omanis were also helped by the degree to which the extensive Portuguese overseas empire had already been weakened by persistent Dutch attacks. Moreover, short of men, ships and money, the Portuguese had only a small military presence on the East African coast. In 1661, the Omanis sacked Mombassa, although they avoided Fort Jesus, the powerful Portuguese fortress there. In 1670, the Omanis pillaged the Portuguese base at Mozambique, but were repulsed by the fortress garrison. The Omanis also pressed the Portuguese in India.

Yet the Omanis did not match the naval range of the Europeans, any more than did the privateers of the Barbary states of North Africa. The Omani impact on India was limited, and their campaigns on the East African coast scarcely revealed a major power. Fort Jesus fell in 1698, but the siege had lasted since 1696 and the Omanis had no siege artillery. The Portuguese, instead, were weakened by beri-beri and other diseases that killed nine-tenths of the garrison, a fate that matched those of their troops in the colony of Mozambique. Nevertheless, Omani pressure, like that of the Mughal ruler Aurangzeb against the English East India Company's base at Bombay in 1686, which led the governor to submit, is a reminder that the narrative of military effectiveness and success is complex, and thus that an analysis predicated on European capability and development is questionable, Whiggish and teleological.

This point is the key element of the global context that has to be recalled. To do so avoids the teleology created by an account of the period from the perspective of eventual European dominance, or indeed from the perspective of the late-eighteenth century when the relative European position was stronger. In contrast, in the seventeenth century, the Europeans only made important inroads where native peoples were fewer, notably in eastern North America, where the English and French established an expanding presence, and in Siberia, across which the Russians advanced to the Pacific Ocean.

Turning to the close of the period covered by this chapter, the American and French Revolutions raise a fundamental exclamation mark against the notion that this period essentially represented a continuation to that of the last chapter. Nevertheless, there were significant continuities in the period of this chapter that helped condition the nature of conflict in practice. These continuities even extend to the American and French revolutions which can be detached from a secular context and seen as another set of the ideological struggles akin to the Wars of Religion. The basic military continuities were provided by the West's dominance of naval power, but not of most of the land, especially in Africa and East Asia; as well as the extent to which China was still the leading military power; the limited resources available for warfare from low-productivity agrarian economies; and the limited skills base of societies in which education and literacy were restricted.

As far as fighting was concerned, there was a change of emphasis for infantry from a role for edged cutting/slashing/stabbing weapons to firearms, in part due to the development and diffusion of bayonets, although European cavalry retained the sword as a primary weapon of shock well into the twentieth century, the carbine being a resort when they had to fight on foot. In terms of technique, this use of muskets equipped with bayonets represented a military transformation, as all infantry could now be armed with a weapon that was defensive as well as offensive. Moreover, firepower was enhanced by the shift from matchlock to flintlock muskets. The switch-over was near total for infantry in Europe, but, because the diffusion of the new weapon was limited on the world scale, this can only be described as a change of emphasis.

Indeed, on the world scale, a continuity in fighting methods is readily apparent. There were differences, for example, between the Manchu invasion of China in the mid-seventeenth century and those of the Mongols four centuries earlier, but they were far less pronounced than those with the British attacks on China in 1839–42 and 1856–60, let alone the Japanese invasion of 1931–45. The same point can be made about conflict in Africa. In Europe, there were contrasts, but again they should not be exaggerated. The close-packed archers of the 1340s were more similar to their musketeer colleagues of the 1790s than the latter were to infantrymen in 1918. At sea, warships remained dependent on wind or rowers, and fought in close proximity, totally unlike battleship battles notably Tsushima (1905) and Jutland (1916), although the last two were line-of-battle engagements similar to those of earlier naval battles.

If continuity is the key characteristic, there were still important developments as a result of conflict. These developments included struggles for naval and colonial mastery between the European powers, struggles that were different, both in scale and in centrality to war goals, from those prior to the mid-seventeenth century. The first key struggle, that between the Dutch and Portuguese, a struggle which was mostly waged in the South Atlantic and around the Indian Ocean, was focused on the drive for profit from trade and colonies. This drive was also a key issue in the three Anglo-Dutch wars in 1652–74, which were waged in West Africa, North America and Guiana, as well as in European waters.

Commercial and colonial profit were also important, albeit less consistently, in the Anglo-French wars, especially the Seven Years' War of 1756–63, a conflict known in the United States as the French and Indian War. These wars called on a range of warmaking, not only the high-spectrum conflict of specialized warships landing regulars, for example the British troops who captured Havana and Manila from France's ally Spain in 1762, but also the employment of local militia as well as of allied units, such as Native Americans. These campaigns, and the related development of military capacity and infrastructure, provided an example of the ability of the European system to adapt to new tasks. The campaigns also delivered results, including the English capture of Dutch North America, New Amsterdam becoming New York in 1664, the British conquest of New France (Québec) in 1759–60, and the French intervention on behalf of the American Revolutionaries, an intervention that brought success at

Yorktown in 1781 with the surrender to George Washington of an outnumbered, besieged and blockaded British army under Charles, Earl Cornwallis.

If these overseas operations provided an example of flexibility and adaptability, another instance was offered by the development by the Austrians and, even more, the Russians, of techniques that could be used in order to defeat Ottoman forces. This development involved devising tactics for effective advances, combining infantry mobility with the firepower produced by close-order discipline, volley fire and flintlocks, in deployments able to hold off the cavalry attacks and enveloping manoeuvres to which the Ottomans habitually resorted. The result was Russian success in a series of wars. The Russians had been defeated at the River Pruth in 1711, but, thereafter, were consistently successful in a series of wars, in part due to an improvement in their ability to mobilize resources from near the zone of operations, a product of their success in transforming Ukraine governmentally, politically, socially and, to a degree with Russian settlement, ethnically.

This success was particularly prominent in the 1768–74 conflict, in which Count Peter Rumyantsev advanced south of the River Danube, breaching the Ottoman fortress system on the Danube, while in 1770 a Russian fleet destroyed its Ottoman opponent off Cesmé in the Aegean. This victory really marked the beginning of the 'Eastern Question', the concern over the fate of the Ottoman Empire that was subsequently to be so important to European international relations. The Russians were to be victorious anew over the Ottomans in 1787–92, 1806–12 and 1826–8, advancing repeatedly south of the Danube while developing a major naval capacity on the Black Sea. Such an account, however, overlooks the extent to which the Russians, and, by extension, this instance of Western warmaking, still faced serious problems. Russian operations against the Ottomans revealed grave flaws, not least in logistics, especially during the 1806–12 war, but the key element was the Russian ability to secure success.

Austrian conflicts with the Ottomans had a more mixed outcome, with the Austrians highly successful in 1683–97 and 1716–8, but defeated in 1737–9. Nevertheless, there was a definite shift between the Austrians successfully resisting Ottoman advances, most obviously in 1664 and 1683, to the Ottomans seeking to check Austrian attacks as in 1695–6 and 1716–8. This shift was a key aspect of the degree to which European forces were increasingly successful against non-Western opponents. Austrian victory at Belgrade in 1717 was important (although some of its consequences were reversed in 1739), as, at a far smaller scale, was that of the British, under Robert Clive, over the Nawab of Bengal at Plassey in 1757. Until the latter, there had been little success on land to report for the Europeans in populated areas of Asia or indeed Africa, but the British victories in India were the first to change this situation.

In contrast to the Balkans, the boundary elsewhere between Islam and Christendom was quieter than had been the case in the sixteenth century. There was conflict in North Africa and the Mediterranean, with Spanish attacks on Algiers unsuccessful, culminating in failure in 1784, but this conflict was not on the same scale as that in the Balkans. This was part of the shift from the Mediterranean as a centre of power and also of military history. The key drivers of naval capability and conflict were now the Atlantic states, while, on land, the centre of European campaigning was no longer around the Mediterranean. Instead, the history of warfare in Europe is written around Gustavus Adolphus of Sweden, Louis XIV of France, Prince Eugene of Austria, John, Duke of Marlborough of Britain, Peter the Great of Russia, Marshal Saxe of France and Frederick the Great of Prussia. Their armies and campaigning constituted *ancien régime* warfare, and it was this that was challenged, first by the American Revolution (1775–83) and then, more directly and in a more sustained fashion, in the French Revolutionary and Napoleonic Wars (1792–1815).

In this period, command became increasingly separated from rule, as demonstrated by Turenne (a marshal for Louis XIV), Eugene,

Marlborough and Saxe. Furthermore, egalitarian and democratic ideals began to influence historical events, as the careers of both Oliver Cromwell, a key Parliamentary general in the English Civil War, and George Washington showed. Nevertheless, military command was a key aspect of rulership. John Campbell's comment on Frederick William I of Prussia (r. 1713–40) – 'he made his troops his delight, and led all his days rather a military than a Court life' – could have been repeated for other rulers. Moreover, many of the key commanders of the period were also rulers. Most, such as Gustavus Adolphus, Peter the Great, Frederick the Great and the Qianlong Emperor of China, inherited the right to rule, and then used war to enhance their assets, Peter, in particular, transforming both army and state in order to increase military effectiveness. In contrast, Nader Shah of Persia took over a failing empire in the 1730s and gave it a military dynamism until his assassination in 1747, but it became less common to create a new empire through war, as Napoleon was to seek to do in the 1800s.

A common requirement of the ruler-leaders in this era was the demonstration of both political and military skill, with the latter closely associated with the former. Thus, it was necessary to divide opponents, to create tensions in their alliances and to fight them in sequence. This was a practice at which Frederick the Great was adept, and at which Napoleon was successful until 1812. It was also import-ant to hold together constituencies of interest, be they alliances, as with Marlborough and the War of the Spanish Succession (1702–13), in which he held together Britain, Austria and the Dutch, or the groups within countries backing a war effort. Victory brought prestige and this, in turn, was important in maintaining political support. Thus, glory, honour and prestige were far from irrational pursuits. Instead, they were the basis of power and authority, conferring a mantle of success and magnificence. In contrast to today, the gains and *gloire* to be won from war were readily identified and eagerly sought.

Gains and *gloire*, however, had a heavy human cost. Marlborough's victories became most costly, with the casualties at Malplaquet in 1709 proving savage and politically contentious. These losses reflected the ability of the French generals to learn how to respond to his tactics, a classic instance of the closing of a capability gap. Civilians were also hit by war. In 1713, when a large Russian amphibious force appeared off Helsinki the greatly outnumbered Swedish garrison burned the town to the ground and ordered the population to leave. In turn, the Russian occupiers of Helsinki from 1713 to 1721 built fortifications, desecrated the graveyard and seized people for Russian service, leading to the period being known as the Great Wrath.

As far as fighting methods were concerned, European warfare can be seen in terms of an action–reaction pattern of development, with leaders creating opportunities and responding to deficiencies, but, in another light, as already indicated, the basic context was one of continuity. If Marlborough smashed through the French centre in successive victories (Blenheim 1704 Ramillies 1706, Oudenaarde 1708), and Frederick the Great devised the tactic of the oblique attack, as at the expense of the Austrians at Leuthen (1757), then they did so with essentially the same forces as their opponents.

Similarity, however, can conceal important contrasts. The tactical flexibility displayed by eighteenth-century generals, in comparison with their seventeenth-century predecessors, owed much to the replacement of the musket/pike combination by the flintlock-bayonet soldiers. In place of the chequerboard formations, came linear ones. By the 1790s, these were to seem rigid and inflexible in comparison to the columns of the Revolutionary French, but that perspective underplays the ability of generals in the 1700 and 1740s (during the Wars of the Spanish and Austrian Successions), especially Marlborough, Eugene, Frederick the Great and Saxe, to deliver victories in a way that had not proved possible in the 1690s. There were also major advances in Europe in artillery: in the understanding of ballistics, in gunfounding and in organization, especially in standardization. The application of new knowledge was a key theme in European military development.

At sea, the capacity to deliver victory also became more prominent. The major British victories of 1794–1805 were prefigured against the French in 1747 (the two Battles of Cape Finisterre), 1759 (Battles of Lagos and Quiberon Bay) and 1782 (the Saintes). Within the continuing constraints of sail, wind, current and direct gunfire, warships were employed more effectively, in both tactical and operational terms. Design improvements, not least based on a greater understanding of hydrostatics and ship stability, enhanced seaworthiness, while better guns and gun-drill increased firepower. The British proved particularly adept at the latter, but their naval superiority was due not to better ships but to a stronger national commitment to sea power.

This British superiority can be dated from the major British victory over the French at Barfleur in 1692, a victory which ended the risk of an invasion on behalf of the exiled James II, who had been driven from England by a Dutch invasion backed up by significant domestic support in the Glorious Revolution of 1688–9. When it came to the crunch, the French, faced in the early 1690s and 1700s with onerous wars on land with a coalition of powers (in which the key partners were Austria, the Dutch and Britain), chose not to invest to maintain their naval strength. In contrast, the British navy rested on a solid basis of political support that was as much a matter of public backing as of governmental. That support did not prevent controversies when failure occurred as over the Battles of Toulon (1744) and Ushant (1778) and the failure to relieve Minorca in 1756, but these controversies were also a response to public support.

Political backing meant money, but this money was available due to the extent of British overseas trade, and the consequent customs revenue and ability to raise loans. Naval strength was significant as it secured this trade, and there was therefore a symbiotic relationship between commerce and naval power. This relationship represented a different cost-benefit analysis for force and war to that represented by armies and their ability to conquer territory. This difference might seem to differentiate Britain from the bulk of

European and non-European powers, but there were also similarities. This situation was especially notable in India in the case of the East India Company and the local powers. The Company's logic was commercial, but it developed a large army of local troops and used it, like a local power, to secure and conquer territory, especially in Bengal, from which it could derive revenue and exert power. This policy looked towards the later development of British imperialism in India and elsewhere.

Militarily, the British in India were the most successful of the transoceanic European powers. Operating in a region in which the demographic situation was very adverse (the British, in contrast, were not outnumbered by Native Americans in the contact zone in North America), and without any levelling up from disease (as there had been for the Spaniards in Mexico, where smallpox killed many of the Aztecs), the British were opposed by dynamic local powers, especially, but not only, the Maratha Confederation in west India and the Sultans of Mysore in south India. The British were also affected by the willingness of France to intervene against them in India. The British had to turn to local manpower, the source of most of the army of the East India Company, although regular units of the British army were an important core, while, at sea, the overwhelming reliance was on the Royal Navy. Local manpower was provided in two forms, first sepoys, Indians trained to fight like European regulars, and, secondly, allied units, for example from the Nizam of Hyderabad in the 1790s, which were especially important as a source of cavalry.

British conquests lead to an assumption of military superiority, not least because the most famous battles – Arcot (1750) and Plassey (1757) – were British victories, which, respectively, established their position in the Carnatic (south-east India) and Bengal; but the situation was less happy as far as the commanders of the time were concerned, and Plassey anyway was a relatively small-scale clash with the major dynamic provided by the British ability to employ bribery to divide the opposing forces. There were serious British failures, not least the Convention of Wadgaon in 1779, by which a

Company army, retreating from an unsuccessful attempt to capture the Maratha capital, Pune (Poona), accepted humiliating terms from the Marathas in order to extricate itself; as well as the defeat of a square of regulars by Mysore forces at Perumbakam in 1780.

Far from British-trained infantry being obviously superior, it proved difficult, especially operationally but also tactically, to overcome the challenge posed by Maratha and Mysore cavalry. When cavalry was combined with artillery, in which the Marathas were proficient, this posed a particular challenge, as for the British at the Battle of Assaye in 1803, where the Duke of Wellington's victory was especially hard fought, leading to high casualty figures. The British advantages were not so much point-of-contact ones on the battlefield, as organizational elements, notably the continuity represented by the Company's structure, when contrasted with the more personal political structures of Indian states.

The British also benefited financially from the Company's commercial strength which, in turn, was a product of maritime range. This strength gave the Company a comparative advantage over its Indian opponents, and another stemmed from Britain's presence in three parts of the sub-continent (with the three bases at Bombay, Calcutta and Madras), and the resulting ability to provide mutual support. The resources of Bengal proved especially valuable when the Bombay Presidency was put under great pressure from the Marathas in 1779, and also helped Madras resist pressure from Mysore.

The British challenge to India's rulers was therefore different from that posed by each other and by non-Western invaders. Both the latter challenges in part arose from the weakness of the power and authority of the Mughal Emperors in the eighteenth century, and the resulting opportunity and need for others to come to the fore. In this situation, outside pressure could no longer be so successfully resisted. Whereas, in the 1620s–50s, Persian expansion had been contested by the Mughals round Kandahar (in modern Afghanistan), in 1739 Nader Shah of Persia was able to invade northern India. He defeated the Mughals at Karnal near Delhi and captured the city, returning home with vast loot including the Peacock Throne. In 1761, the Afghan invaders of northern India were resisted not by the Mughals but by the Marathas, then India's leading military power, who, however, were thoroughly beaten in the Third Battle of Panipat, the largest engagement of the century. These invasions helped explain why Indian rulers did not put the British and French foremost among their opponents and also why their force structures were designed to oppose armies dominated by cavalry which was a different threat from that from the British.

This reminder of the difference of military tasks that might be encountered in the same area can be repeated with reference to North America where European forces had to be able to confront not only each other but also Native Americans, and the same was also true for the latter. The geographical focus was pertinent, with European v. European conflict central in the coastal littoral, and conflict with Native Americans central in the interior. Neither type of conflict was uniform or unchanging and there were also overlapping elements, not least the role of fortifications. Yet, reference to forts also underlines the difference because they played a contrasting role in conflict with other Europeans from that in warfare with Native Americans. The taking of key positions ended the resistance of France in Canada in 1760, and the war between Britain and France in North America centred on forts: Louisbourg, Ticonderoga, Québec and Montréal, with St Augustine and later Pensacola playing a comparable role for Britain and Spain. The major battles fought by European forces outside Europe continued to be against other European forces, notably in North America. The scale of conflict was different in the case of Europeans against the Native Americans as was the practice of fortification, but the seizure and burning of Native villages could be important to their defeat, while the European presence in frontier areas was anchored by fortifications.

The violent nature of the North American background was important to the creation in the American Revolution (1775–85) of a military system – the Continental Army and state militia – able to engage with the British regulars. Not only had many Americans already engaged in military operations, but there were also, in the shape of the colonial militia, practices and institutions of co-operation. Yet, the process of transfer of these capabilities to a new military system was not without serious problems, not least because of the difficulties of trying to enforce obligations in the anti-authoritarian context of a revolution against British authority. As a result, the extent to which the Americans were able to take the initiative in 1775 and early 1776 was important. The British had not anticipated a revolution across the Thirteen Colonies that became the basis of the United States, and the British forces available were too few and, anyway, were concentrated in Massachusetts. As a consequence, British authority elsewhere collapsed. The failure, at the Battle of Bunker Hill (1775), to crush the American army outside Boston also created an impression that the Americans would succeed.

What the Americans had failed to anticipate sufficiently was the extent to which the British would not settle politically but, instead, would mount a major effort in 1776 to re-establish their position. Indeed, the ability of imperial powers to draw on wider resources in responding to rebellions was a key aspect in the failure of many rebellions, as with those against British rule, notably of the Jacobites in Scotland in 1745–6 and the Indian Mutiny in 1857–9. Similarly in Corsica: the French purchase of the Mediterranean island from Genoa in 1768 led to resistance to French occupation. Corsican resolve, knowledge of the terrain and fighting qualities, combined with French over-confidence and poor planning, resulted in Corsican successes, but, in 1769–70, larger French forces, better tactics and the use of devastation, terror and road construction produced success. The French also benefited from the absence of foreign military support for the Corsicans. Corsica was incorporated into France, making a French subject of Napoleone di Buonaparte, who was born in 1769.

In the case of North America, the British were helped by the extent to which, unlike when attacking the French in North America in the 1690 1700s 1740s and 1750s, they were not having to operate in Europe in 1775–7. Partly as a result, in 1776, the empire hit back. An amphibious force relieved the garrison at Québec from American siege, another tried (but failed) to capture a key fort off Charleston and the main effort was mounted against New York. The British defeated the Continental Army under George Washington at Long Island, before mounting a successful amphibious assault on Manhattan. The defeated Americans fell back, losing troops through desertion, and the British successfully advanced across New Jersey.

At Christmas 1776, Washington, in turn, hit back, crossing the icy Delaware River by night, and surprising and defeating a Hessian force in British service at Trenton. In hindsight, this victory represented a crucial turning point in the war, as the British lost the impetus and the impression of success. In more specific terms, Trenton was followed by a British withdrawal in New Jersey and ensured that when the British advance on Philadelphia, the meeting place of the Continental Congress, resumed in 1777, the British did not feel confident that they would be able to mount this successfully overland via New Jersey. Instead, in what turned out to be a highly disjointed strategy, lacking a concentration of effort, the main army under Sir William Howe slowly sailed to Chesapeake Bay, landed and advanced on Philadelphia, outflanking and defeating a defending army at Brandywine Creek. This approach, however, ensured that Howe's force was unable to support the other major British army under John Burgoyne which advanced south from Canada along the axis of the River Hudson in an attempt to cut the Thirteen Colonies in half by separating New England from the rest. In the face of increasingly larger American forces, this plan proved a rash choice because Burgoyne was isolated. Blocked in hilly wooded terrain west of the Hudson, and unable to break through the American positions, Burgoyne's force surrendered at Saratoga.

A military account of the struggle begs the question whether the British, anyway, could have prevailed over the Americans; in short whether the very act of revolution led to its success, as John Adams, a prominent revolutionary, later suggested. This is an important question that is more generally relevant for warfare, and notably so in insurgency/counter-insurgency struggles in which an appreciable percentage of the population are politically aware. If the defeat of an opponent is seen as in part requiring their acceptance that they have been defeated, then the degree of will shown in rejecting that conclusion is crucial.

In the case of the American Revolution, this is especially important because the British government did not want, and could not afford, a large occupation force. Instead, like most imperial powers, its rule depended on consent, and, in the case of the Thirteen Colonies, especially so as this was a civil war the solution to which was seen by contemporaries as political as much as military. The understanding of this may make British warmaking seem modern, involving as it did hearts and minds, but in practice this technique was common to counter-revolutionary warfare when the revolution, far from being restricted to marginal groups in society, included the socially prominent.

Moreover, as Philip II of Spain had shown when responding unsuccessfully to the Dutch Revolt in the late-sixteenth century, the availability of a linked political-military strategy did not guarantee success. So also with the American Revolution. The Continental Congress rejected negotiations and the British found it difficult to build up the strength of their Loyalist supporters. Yet, the American Patriots or revolutionaries also found the war an increasingly difficult conflict and, by 1781, their war effort was close to collapse, with much of the Continental Army mutinous and the government desperately short of money.

Moreover, the American effort was in part dependent on the international context. In 1778, France came into the war against Britain, but by 1781 it was clear that the French government was looking for a way out. In the event, Franco-American co-operation against a poorly situated British army in 1781 led to the surrender of the latter at Yorktown. This defeat still left the British in control of New

York, Charleston and Savannah, but it produced a crisis of confidence in the ministry in Britain, and a new government came to power pledged to negotiate with the Americans. Again, this brought out a key element in such insurrectionary conflicts: as the Americans were not in a position to invade Britain, the war could only come to an end when the British decided to cease making an effort, and this again had a strong political dimension.

The international dimension of insurrectionary conflicts also emerged clearly. The Americans were heavily dependent on the French at Yorktown, not only on French troops and, crucially, artillery on land, but also on the ability of the French navy, in the Battle of the Virginia Capes, to block the entrance to Chesapeake Bay to British warships and thus to prevent the relief of the British force. This point also underlines the danger of thinking of this war in telelogical terms: of the defeat of an *ancien régime* (old regime) army by a revolutionary new force. The French military scarcely conformed to this model, while, indeed, the Continental Army owed its tactics and structure to the general Western model. Guerrilla warfare tended to occur only when American regular forces were very weak, as in the South in 1781.

Britain's naval failure off the Chesapeake in 1781 was rectified the following year with a crushing victory over the French off the Saintes in the West Indies in 1782. This victory not only blocked French plans in the West Indies but was also part of a more general situation in which the British failure in the Thirteen Colonies was not matched by a wider collapse of the empire, in part due to the strength of the Royal Navy. Despite also being at war with France, Spain (from 1779), the Dutch (from 1780) and the Marathas and Mysore in India, Britain held off most of the attacks. There were losses in the Mediterranean (Minorca) and the Caribbean (with Spain conquering West Florida and France seizing some islands); but Canada was held against American attack and Gibraltar against Spanish siege, and a Franco-Spanish invasion attempt on southern England in 1779 failed due to delay and disease. George Washington's plan to capture New York in 1782 could not be implemented, not least due to a lack of French support.

This conflict indicated the extent to which *ancien régime* warfare was neither limited nor static. Instead, it spanned much of the world, with bold attempts at power projection, such as the French fleet and army sent to India in 1780. British resilience was also a key dimension. As with much else, this resilience, like the global range of the war, linked the French Revolutionary War with what came earlier.

Breaking out in 1789, the French Revolution was in part a product of military failure, as was shown in two respects. First, the French government had badly lost domestic prestige as a result of military failure, both defeat in battle, notably Rossbach at the hands of Frederick the Great of Prussia in 1757, and an inability to confront Prussia and Britain in the Dutch Revolt of 1787. The latter was an episode that fell short of war but where equations of military strength, international support and political resolution, all proved mutually supporting. Second, despite considering doing so in 1789, the French government did not use the army to suppress disaffection and opposition. Indeed, the opposite occurred: the army was unable to maintain order and prevent violent insurrectionary episodes, and notably so in the centre of government, Paris, in 1789 and 1792.

An increasingly more radical government and politics in France led to the mustering of a counter-revolutionary coalition, and war broke out in 1792. Initially, it seemed that the Revolution might fail, with Prussian and Austrian forces successfully invading eastern France; but, already facing serious logistical problems, especially in food supplies, the Prussians under Charles, Duke of Brunswick were checked at Valmy by a larger French army supported by effective artillery and then fell back. The French forces exploited the situation in late 1792, successfully invading the Rhineland, Belgium and Savoy (then part of Piedmont). This exploitation was a victory for larger numbers, for the potential they offered for the battlefield tactic of a bold advance employing columns of massed infantry, as at Jemappes, the battle that led to the overrunning of Belgium, and for political resolution. In contrast, there was a degree of uncertainty about opposition to the French, especially on the part of the Prussians; and Prussia, Austria and, in particular, Russia all proved more interested in partitioning Poland out of existence in 1793 and 1795, with Russia playing the key role in suppressing opposition.

By 1796, despite Britain, the Dutch and Spain entering the war against France in 1793, the French had conquered the Low Countries and western Germany (then divided among a large number of German principalities), and had knocked Prussia and Spain out of the opposing coalition. In 1797, Austria was forced to accept terms, in particular as a result of Napoleon's repeated defeat of Austrian forces in northern Italy, in battles such as Lodi, and his subsequent advance towards Austria.

These victories are easier to list than to explain, in part because a number of possible explanations have been offered. These range from tactical, specifically the superiority of French columns over their opponents' lines of troops, to organizational, especially the division system and the provision of plentiful artillery, to numbers – the large number of troops produced by the conscription of the *levée en masse*, and to the enthusiasm of a popular revolution. These explanations are all subsumed for many by the argument that the French represented a modern and modernizing way of war, one characterized by total goals and means, not least a mobilization of all the resources of society. In turn, this analysis is held to explain success over *ancien régime* states and militaries that lacked such resolution and effort, and whose warmaking was characterized accordingly.

While apparently persuasive, many aspects of this interpretation have been picked apart by scholarship concerned to demonstrate the complexity of warmaking in the 1790s, the limitations of French Revolutionary forces and the extent to which they could be defeated. This scholarship is not simply a case of the revenge of the particular on the general, but also raises profound questions about the way in which the image of military change frequently serves as a substitute for reality. For example, alongside the theory of a radical break, it is necessary to note the extent to which the French army was already changing from mid-century, not least in response to failure during the Seven Years' War (1756–63). This change was especially true organizationally and also of the development of an effective artillery, which, indeed, provided Napoleon's background. It would also be inappropriate to argue that the French alone were capable of devising aggressive tactical and operational methods, as the Russian army abundantly showed. Moreover, the British navy was probably the most proficient force in the 1790s (certainly more so than its French counterpart), and it abundantly demonstrated both the value of professionalism and the extent to which success was not dependent on radicalism, in politics or in war.

This navy also enabled Britain to project its power, seizing French colonies in the 1790s and those of the Dutch and Spaniards, such as Cape Town from the Dutch in 1796 and Trinidad from the Spaniards in 1797, once they became France's allies. The strategic and geopolitical consequences of British naval power were more far-ranging. Napoleon struck at Egypt in 1798, in an attempt both to retain his own military position (like Julius Caesar invading Britain in 55 and 54 BCE) and to establish French power on the route to the Orient, which was an aspiration fusing geopolitics and his own image of himself as a latter-day Alexander the Great.

After capturing Alexandria, Napoleon defeated the Mamelukes at Shubra Khit and Embabeh at the Battle of the Pyramids, victories for defensive firepower over the shock tactics of the Mameluke cavalry. Fearing a threat to India, not least because of their struggle with Tipu Sultan of Mysore, the British mounted a powerful riposte. This included Nelson's defeat of the French fleet at the Battle of the Nile (1798) and, after the now isolated Napoleon had abandoned his forces and returned to France in 1799, the landing, in 1801, of a British expeditionary force near Alexandria that defeated the French and forced their surrender.

The ability to combine British forces from both Britain and India in Egypt, and to secure an outcome, was a testimony to a range of power that looked towards more fully-fledged strategies of global power in the two World Wars of the twentieth century. The differences were numerous, but the ability to make such a comparison underlines the unique nature of European warmaking on the world scale. It also suggests that narratives of military modernization should focus on Britain, and not France, and indeed that the key revolution was economic (the Industrial Revolution led by Britain), and not political (the French Revolution). Moreover, if politics is to be emphasized, then the sophistication of a British system capable of ensuring funds, consistency and outcomes without the instability seen in France, deserves emphasis. This system was particularly apparent in the case of the Royal Navy.

Britain in 1800 also exemplified the development of state forms and political institutions over recent centuries, one that had great consequences for military activity. The England of the Wars of the Roses in the late fifteenth century, as well as the Scotland and Ireland of the same period, was a society in which warlords, such as Richard, Earl of Warwick, a real and would-be kingmaker in 1469–71, played a central role: whereas, by 1800, Britain was a state with organizations designed to control violence and to ensure that it was directed only against foreign powers. This monopolization of violence was important to state development and modernization, and helped provide the backdrop to much of nineteenth-century politics and warfare.

The World of the European Empires, 1800–1950

The nineteenth and twentieth centuries defy ready organization. They are at once the age of imperialism and of world wars, of civil conflict on an unprecedented scale and of revolutions. Any one approach risks being misleading. Conventionally, the period is divided at 1914, with a nineteenth century that had begun with Napoleon's defeat at Waterloo in 1815 brought to an end with the outbreak of the First World War. A further division occurs in 1945, to mark the end of the Second World War and the beginning of the Cold War, and another in 1989–91 to mark the end of the Cold War. This approach has value, and echoes of it will be found in this book, but the emphasis, instead, is on a different perspective on the World Question, the issue of primacy in the world. Here the stress is on Western territorial imperialism.

This imperialism neither began in 1800 nor ended in 1950, but that period comprehended the apogee of Western territorial control, and indeed much of its history. In 1799 the British defeated and killed Tipu, Sultan of Mysore, their leading opponent in southern India, when they stormed his capital, Seringapatam, while British naval victories in 1798 (Battle of the Nile) and 1805 (Trafalgar) put paid to any challenge that the French navy might mount to Britain's security and imperial position. After 1950 the Portuguese and French empires continued, while Britain was still a major imperial power east of Suez and in the West Indies, but, by then, the Dutch, French and British had already lost much of the empires they had held or regained control over at the end of the Second World War. A decade later, 1960 saw independence for most of France's possessions in Africa as well as for the Belgian Congo and the British colony of Nigeria.

Rise and fall might thus seem a clear narrative for empire, with the military historian switching from accounts of European military columns and squares under pressure in the African or Afghan sun of the late nineteenth century, to insurgents assaulting European positions in the 1950s in the jungles of Vietnam and Malaya or the arid uplands of Algeria. That approach, however, is also too simple. Indeed, it omits one of the biggest transformations of empire in our period, the collapse of Spanish and Portuguese control in Latin America in the 1820s. This collapse, moreover, can be seen as the result of one of the most significant conflicts of the nineteenth century, not least because it gave shape to a part of the world that has retained the same territorial configuration (and indeed aspects of the politics) to the present day. Moreover, the Latin American Wars of Independence revealed many of the characteristics of more recent insurgency struggles, including the interrelationships with international developments and supporters, the role of political determination and the extent to which the supporters of the opposing side were terrorized. Ethnic tensions also played a major role in the Latin American Wars of Independence.

These Wars of Independence can be seen in a pattern that began with the War of American Independence and continued, in the 1790s, with the revolution in France's leading slave colony, St Dominique, a revolution that led, in 1804, to the establishment of the independent state of Haiti. Yet, in explaining the Latin American Wars of Independence, there is also the key element of developments within Europe, namely the consequences of the French invasion of Portugal in 1807 and, more immediately, Spain in 1808.

This act of dynastic imperialism, for Napoleon put his ineffectual brother Joseph on the throne of Spain, provoked the seizure of power across the empire by *juntas* supportive of the imprisoned king. This seizure accustomed the colonies to self-government and when, from 1814, the restored royal family attempted to reimpose control across Spanish America, it was resisted. Taking place over a far larger area (Mexico to Chile) than the War of American Independence, and lacking the military and political coherence of the latter (there was no equivalent to the Continental Congress or the Continental Army), any description of the Latin American Wars of Independence risks becoming a confused account with rapid changes of fortune. As in the War of American Independence, there was no automatic success for the revolutionary forces, and they were not inherently better than their opponents at combat. Instead, both sides adapted to the issues and problems of conflict across an area in which it was difficult to fix success or indeed to arrange logistical support. Logistical needs helped compromise the popularity of both sides while the expropriation and looting involved inflicted much damage on society. The royalists were also hit by shifts in policy within Spain, which alienated support in Latin America and culminated in a civil war in Spain in 1823. At the same time, fighting ability and command skills, especially those of José de San Martin in Chile in 1817–8 and of Simón Bolívar in northern South America and the Andean chain in 1813–25, were important in wearing down the resistance of the increasingly isolated royalist forces.

The situation in Brazil was different, as the revolution there in the 1820s reflected tensions within the royal family. The resolution also led to conflict within the colony with the need to conquer areas supporting the Crown, which was rapidly achieved. By the end of that decade, European control on the American mainland south of Canada had been reduced to Guiana (British, French and Dutch) and fragments on the coast of Central America, a radical change in global power and one that was not to be reversed. Indeed, the major attempt to do so, France's military intervention in Mexico in the 1860s on behalf of a client ruler, the Emperor Maximilian, proved unsuccessful. In contrast, the United States was in a better position to extend its power and influence. Indeed, Mexico lost much land to the

United States as a result of the Mexican–American War of 1846–8.

Rather, however, than treating the Latin American Wars of Independence as a failure for European power, it would be more accurate to treat them as an aspect of a shift in power within the West. Indeed, they can be seen as part of the consolidation of British strength within the Western world, in this case in an informal empire. British volunteers had played an important role in the struggle, as had British diplomatic and naval support, not least in dissuading possible French intervention on behalf of Spain. Once independent, the Latin American powers which, while colonies, had been excluded from direct trade with Britain, developed close trading relations and also became prime areas for British investment.

Britain, therefore, was the prime beneficiary of the Latin American Wars of Independence, just as its colonial position had improved greatly during the Napoleonic Wars with France and her allies. These conflicts had provided Britain with the opportunity both to seize their colonies, for example Mauritius from France and Cape Colony from the Dutch, and also to pursue wars with non-Western powers with the minimum of interference. The latter was particularly the case in South Asia. The Maratha Confederation was weakened in war in 1803–6, with the future Duke of Wellington's victories at Assaye and Argaum in 1803 proving especially important. The Gurkhas of Nepal were put under considerable pressure in 1814–5, while, in Sri Lanka, the kingdom of Kandy, which had successfully resisted the Portuguese and the Dutch, was conquered in 1815.

Yet such details make the process of imperial expansion overly unproblematic. It is equally of note that the British encountered considerable difficulties in these and other wars. The first war with Kandy, in 1803, was a failure, with British forces in the interior defeated. The Marathas inflicted heavy casualties even when defeated, including a quarter of the British force at Assaye, not least because their artillery was good and they served the guns well. In addition to problems in battle, the British found it difficult to overcome the Marathas, particularly because the latter's force structure included both effective cavalry and impressive fortifications. The British, moreover, were unsuccessful when they intervened in Egypt in 1807 for a similar reason to their failure at Buenos Aires the same year: regulars sent against defended towns lost the advantages of unit cohesion and firepower. It was not till their next military operation against Egypt, in 1882, that the British were victorious.

Rather, therefore, than think in terms of some immutable Western advantage, in the shape of the technologically proficient British, it is more pertinent to note that it proved difficult to translate British naval pre-eminence into success on land. Where success was greatest, in South Asia, it owed much to the organizational factors mentioned in the last chapter that enabled Britain to do well in the military labour market rather than to any particular technological edge on land. In some respects, this situation might appear a 'traditional' form of power, with Britain simply another in a sequence of South Asian empires. In turn, this position could be contrasted with the technologically far more potent Western empires of the late nineteenth century, with their telegraphs, railways and machine guns, their vanquishing of diseases and their ability to conquer lands that had hitherto generally avoided rule, especially direct rule, by foreign empires, for example Vietnam, Burma and most of Africa.

This contrast would be overly simple. Organizational factors could be as modern as technological ones, but, more profoundly, the range, character and maritime basis of Britain's empire in the early nineteenth century was both distinctive and different from that of Asian predecessors and contemporaries. The British empire was also different from that of Napoleon, who gained control of France thanks to a coup in 1799, crowned himself Emperor in 1804 and ruled until 1814, briefly regaining power in 1815. Napoleon's empire was landward and focused on himself. For example giving kingdoms and principalities to his relatives, such as Spain to his brother Joseph in 1808, was scarcely empire on the British pattern. Napoleon's empire was also dedicated to war, while the relationship between war and the British empire was more complex: the British expanded through war, but lacked conscription and the accompanying military ethos, and did not want the expenditure of sustained conflict.

Such cost-benefit analysis was far from Napoleon's priorities. Instead, he saw war as a means to immortality for self, army and nation, and had scant interest in limits, compromise or peace. Whereas Louis XIV had annexed nearby Strasbourg in 1681 and had sought to gain Luxembourg, Napoleon added distant Hamburg (1810) and Rome (1809) to the French Empire, and, in 1812, invaded Russia.

Napoleon dominated the military imagination of the Western world for most of the nineteenth century. This might seem ironic as his career ended in total failure, but Napoleon's generalship was for long held up as the pinnacle of military achievement, and not only by the French. A Corsican who had become a Second Lieutenant in the artillery under Louis XVI, Napoleon's career took off as a result of the French Revolution, which provided many opportunities for talented opportunists like him, not least a major war. Napoleon made his name in 1793 when his successful command of the artillery in the siege of Toulon played a key role in driving British and royalist forces from this crucial Mediterranean port. Promoted to Brigadier General in December 1793, Napoleon was young (born in 1769) and ambitious like many of the Revolutionary generals. He was made artillery commander for the French army in Italy the following February, but he suffered from the political instability in France, being briefly imprisoned in 1794. The following year, Napoleon employed artillery firing at point-blank range, the famous 'whiff of grape-shot', to help put down a rising in Paris. The revolutionary state wielded power internally as it expanded externally.

As a reward, Napoleon was appointed by the grateful government to the command of the Army of Italy. Here, he developed and demonstrated in 1796 the characteristics of his generalship: self-confidence, swift decision-making, rapid mobility, the concentration of strength at what was made the decisive point and, where possible, the exploitation of interior lines. Napoleon's tactical grasp and ability to manoeuvre knocked Sardinia (Piedmont) out of the war and brought repeated victory over the Austrians who dominated northern Italy. His siting of the artillery was particularly important. Victory in northern Italy crucially associated Napoleon with military success and played a central role in the Napoleonic legend; one seen, for example, in the paintings, by David and others, of Napoleon as a bold and glorious leader.

Napoleon's invasion of Egypt in 1798 was less successful, being undercut by the British navy and Nelson's victory at the Battle of the Nile; but in 1799 Napoleon was able to seize power in France with a coup, becoming First Consul and General in Chief. In 1804, he promoted himself to Emperor. As such, he was in a position not only to act as an innovative general, but also to control the French military system and to direct the war effort. Napoleon enjoyed greater power over the army than any French ruler since Louis XIV. Decision-making was concentrated. Furthermore, in many respects, Napoleon was more powerful than Louis. His choice of commanders was not constrained by the social conventions and aristocratic alignments that affected Louis, and both armies and individual military units were under more direct governmental control than had been the case with the Bourbon dynasty. In addition, Napoleon was directly in command of the leading French force throughout the wars of his reign. This underlined his key military role, at once strategic, operational and tactical. Although he had to manage many campaigns from a distance, they were always those of subsidiary forces.

Napoleon concentrated his resources and attention on a single front, seeking in each war to identify the crucial opposing force and to destroy it rapidly. This, not the occupation of territory, was his goal. For temperamental reasons, and because he wanted glory and rapid and decisive results, Napoleon sought battle. He attacked both in campaigning and in battle. Although Napoleon fought for much of his reign, his individual wars with Continental opponents were over fairly rapidly. Warfare (incorporating diplomacy, preparation and the campaign) might be a long-term process for Napoleon, but war became an event. Thus, for example, wars with Austria in 1805 and 1809 ended (victoriously) the same year, while the war with Prussia that began in 1806 ended in 1807. Such rapid results were the product of a concentration of military resources on a single front and a drive for rapid victory in battle and for a speedy follow-through in a quick peace. The Russians, however, proved more intractable, and the peace in 1807 that ended the war started in 1805 reflected, in part, the exhaustion of both sides.

On campaign, Napoleon sought a central position in order to divide more numerous opposing forces and then defeat them separately. A manoeuvrist technique of envelopment was used against weaker forces: they were pinned down by an attack mounted by a section of the French army, while most of the army enveloped them, attacking them in flank or, preferably, cutting their lines of supply and retreat, the *manoeuvre sur les derrières*. This technique put the opponent in a disadvantageous position if they wished to fight on rather than surrender. A similar technique was to be employed by the Prussians under Moltke against the Austrians in 1866 and the French in 1870, again with considerable success.

Napoleon was a strong believer in the value of artillery, organized into strong batteries, particularly of 12-pounders. He increased the number of field guns and the ratio of guns to infantry. Napoleon used his cannon as an offensive force. To do so, he made them as mobile on the battlefield as possible, by the utilization of effective horse-drawn limbers. Napoleon also massed his cavalry for use at the vital moment, and launched large-scale charges when he saw it. In many respects, Napoleon represented the culmination of the military innovations of the French Revolution. He developed the innovations and practices of the 1790s and systematized them. Crucially, however, Napoleon was more successful than his predecessors.

Napoleon confronted grave problems, not least the number and fighting quality of his opponents and the difficulty of establishing their positions, let alone intentions, the primitive communications of the period and the need to raise the operational effectiveness of his conscripts. He deserves credit for developing an effective army, but he was unable to match his political goals to the reality of a complex international system with which he needed to compromise were he to maintain his position.

When Napoleon seized power in 1799, Revolutionary France was already at war and under considerable pressure from the Second Coalition, and, crucially, the combination of Austria, Britain and Russia. Boldly advancing into Italy, Napoleon regained the initiative, winning a hard-fought battle at Marengo. This was a battle, like many, in which a capacity to respond to the unexpected and to fight through was crucial. The fighting quality of the experienced French forces proved important, not least the ability to keep going in adverse circumstances. Rather than seeing this ability in terms of any particular characteristics of the French army, however, it is worth noting that the same was true, for example, of Wellington's victories over the Marathas in 1803.

French successes led to the dissolution of the Second Coalition, with Russia coming to terms in 1800, Austria in 1801 and Britain in 1802. Napoleon was left dominant in Western Europe, but his determination to gain advantages from the peace, his clear preparations for fresh conflict and his inability to pursue measures likely to encourage confidence led to a resumption of conflict with Britain in 1803. In turn, British efforts, not least the payment of subsidies, resulted in the creation of the Third Coalition.

This alliance was a formidable combination, but also suffered from a lack of organizational cohesion or unity, as well as poor planning and communications. Partly as a result, it proved easier for Napoleon to respond rapidly to circumstances, which he did in 1805 by advancing east, outmanoeuvring and forcing the surrender of an Austrian army at Ulm, before destroying an Austro-Russian army at Austerlitz: Napoleon proved a master not only of gaining the initiative through rapid campaigning, but also of moving large forces on the battlefield. Napoleon's mastery of logistics was superior to that of his opponents. In 1806, the Prussians were knocked out at Jena, while in 1807 the Russians agreed terms. Napoleon was left dominant in Central Europe, a situation underlined when Austria was defeated afresh in 1809, with Prussia and Russia looking on.

Yet, the weaknesses of Napoleon's empire, both politically and militarily, were already apparent. The rising in Spain in 1808 against newly asserted French control indicated that the policies and politics on offer from Napoleon were scarcely going to assuage opposition. Instead, Napoleon was widely seen as an unwelcome imperialist, and this served to prefigure the extent to which the new empires created in the nineteenth century found it difficult to win a strong foundation of support, with the exception of those, such as the United States in the American West and Argentina in the Pampas, able to rely on demographic advantage, an advantage expressed in land seizure and settlement.

The rising in Spain also demonstrated a potential for popular action and irregular forces that was to be seen elsewhere. Thus, in 1798, after Napoleon had captured Malta en route to Egypt, a popular insurrection against the policies of the new radical regime overran much of the island and confined the French to a few positions, although their surrender in 1800 also owed much to a British naval blockade. The unpopularity both of the French Revolutionaries and of Napoleon led to a series of risings against both.

Napoleon was totally unable to command success at sea, and the impact of the French and allied navies under his control proved far less than the sum of their parts. Although he made major efforts to rebuild the French navy after its defeat by the British at Trafalgar in 1805, he was short of sailors, and his navy crucially lacked the experience that was so important to British success. On land, battles like Marengo had indicated that French victories could be very hard won, and Napoleon encountered severe difficulties fighting the Russians at Eylau and Friedland in 1807 and the Austrians at Aspern-Essling in 1809. The extent to which his opponents were able to copy successfully such French organizational innovations as the corps system is controversial, but it is clear that their fighting quality was such that French relative advantages were limited.

The consequences of this became rapidly apparent when Napoleon lost control of the political situation with his invasion of Russia in 1812. This invasion was strategically naive as it was already clear from Spain in 1808 that a successful advance culminating in the capture of the opposing capital was not sufficient to lead to the overawing of the other side, a lesson driven home when the British briefly occupied Washington in 1814 during the Anglo-American 'War of 1812' (in fact of 1812–5). After eventually winning a hard-fought battle at Borodino, a battle in which he resorted to costly frontal attacks, Napoleon captured an abandoned Moscow, but Tsar Alexander I proved unwilling to negotiate, and, under heavy Russian pressure, the French army disintegrated on its retreat through the frozen winter landscape.

Defeat in Russia encouraged those unwillingly allied to Napoleon to turn against him. As a result, an outnumbered Napoleon was defeated by Austrian, Prussian, Russian and Swedish forces at Leipzig in 1813, the Battle of the Nations. No battle in Europe had seen so many troops and cannon on the battlefield, and Napoleon's defeat was followed by his loss of Germany, and, in 1814, by the successful Allied invasion of France, culminating in the occupation of Paris and in Napoleon's enforced abdication.

Meanwhile, British forces sent to help Portuguese and Spanish resistance to France had, from 1808, inflicted a series of defeats, most prominently Salamanca (1812) and Vitoria (1813). These victories indicated the extent to which the French could be outfought on the battlefield, and led to the French being driven from Spain. This process of outfighting the French culminated at Waterloo in 1815 when Napoleon, having returned from exile, invaded Belgium, attacking an Anglo-Dutch-German army under the Duke of Wellington. Relying on the defensive firepower and determination of his British infantry, Wellington beat back a series of disjointed and poorly executed attacks before a Prussian force arrived to attack Napoleon's flank.

The French army disintegrated and Napoleon fled. Surrendering to a British warship, he was held on the British-ruled South Atlantic island of St Helena until he died, his fate a clear demonstration of British power. Napoleon had had to be outfought: as with Germany in the two World Wars, he was not simply defeated as a result of the greater resources of his opponents.

The struggle between Britain and France represented a major shift in the nature of European power. The Mediterranean, where Britain captured Malta from France in 1800, had become a front line between the alliance systems of two clashing empires, as it was to be again with the First World War and, far more clearly and significantly, with the Second World War. Unlike, however, the clash between Rome and Carthage or that of Venice and the Ottomans, this was not a struggle controlled by Mediterranean powers. Instead, it was one in which the Mediterranean was understood in terms of geopolitical axes devised by strategists in distant capitals and its resources were used to support their strategies. This situation helps to explain the French invasion of Spain in 1808, and the British counter-intervention, as well as the campaigning of both powers in southern Italy and in the Adriatic. A British force landed in Calabria in 1806, attacking the French, the only British invasion of southern Italy prior to that in 1943 during the Second World War. To the British troops who defeated the French at Maida in Calabria in 1806, this expedition must have seemed as distant as the Roman legionaries had found Britannia.

The Napoleonic Wars dominated the Western military imagination until the 1860s. The two leading military intellectuals of the century, Clausewitz and Jomini, served in them, as did many of the generals who held command into mid-century, for example the Austrian Radetzky. The lessons learned, or at least the experience gained, proved useful, as with the Austrian suppression of opposition in Italy in 1820–1. Yet, the Napoleonic Wars were of less benefit for European operations overseas. Indeed, the Napoleonic-style formations and operations used by the French in Algeria in the

1830s in an attempt to overcome Muslim opposition to French expansion had to be replaced by more flexible methods, not least raids by cavalry columns. The British also used Napoleonic (or rather Wellingtonian)-style formations and operations overseas, but they encountered severe problems when up against firm opposition, as in the two Sikh Wars of the 1840s, although they ultimately defeated the Sikhs, greatly strengthening their position in northern India.

The most successful British operations were those in which they could employ their unmatched naval superiority. Thus, in the First Burmese War (1824–6), operations were able to be extended from the Arakan borderlands of Burma and India to hit at the centres of Burmese power by means of amphibious strikes, first at Rangoon and then up the River Irrawaddy. In the latter, as in the First Opium War with China of 1838–42, the British made use of the capacity that steam power brought to naval operations in coastal and inland waters. Amphibious attacks led to the seizure of Chinese ports, and then the British advanced against Nanjing, using their naval strength to provide not only lift, logistics and firepower, but also to cut Chinese grain supplies. The Chinese agreed to terms, ceding Hong Kong.

This acquisition appears a brilliant success but, in part, it was dependent on limited British goals, which did not include extensive conquest, and on weak Chinese leadership. Had a ruler of the calibre of the Kangzi Emperor (see pp. 84–5) been in charge, then resistance would probably have continued and it would have been difficult for the British to force the Chinese to settle. Similar points can be made in the case of the Second Opium or Arrow War (1858–60), in which British forces occupied Beijing in 1860. In the latter case, the British were helped by the extent to which China was divided and weakened by the extensive and lengthy (but ultimately unsuccessful) Taipeng Rebellion. Similarly, Chinese resistance to the Manchus in the 1640s and to the Japanese in the 1930s was weakened by civil war.

While seeking a monopoly, direct or indirect, over the means of coercion, empire was also dependent on local co-operation, a point driven home for Britain by the problems encountered in overcoming the Indian Mutiny of 1857–9, a rebellion made particularly serious by the involvement of large numbers of Britain's Indian forces. In turn, the willingness of others to remain loyal, as well as the support provided by allied Indian rulers, especially those of Hyderabad, Kashmir and Nepal, were important in defeating the Mutiny, although British regulars also played a major role in what was very hard fighting.

Whether overseas or in Europe, much of the fighting in mid-century was at relatively close-quarters, with units able to see whom they were shooting at, and with the opportunity for bayonet advances. This was true not only of the fighting in India, but also of that in Europe provoked by the Year of Revolutions (1848) and by the Franco-Austrian War of 1859 fought in northern Italy, especially in the bloody battles of Magenta and Solferino. The casualties in the latter inspired the foundation of the Red Cross. This close-quarter fighting was also to be the dominant mode of combat in the American Civil War (1861–5), and helps explain the high casualty rates to which it led. The consequences of close-quarter fighting were exacerbated by improvements in the lethality of artillery and of hand-held firearms. The rapid fire of rifles made the massed infantry assaults of the Civil War very costly.

Greater and more predictable production of munitions, not least of interchangeable weapon components, flowed from a more streamlined and systematized manufacturing process. The overall result was a degree of change far greater in pace and scope than that over the previous century. Land warfare was transformed by the continual incremental developments in firearms, such as the introduction of the percussion rifle and the Minié bullet, both in the 1840s, and, subsequently, of breech-loading cartridge rifles. Rifling increased accuracy and range, while breech-loading led to more rapid fire. Breech-loading had long been available but, to be effective and lethal it required a metal centrefire cartridge, smokeless propellants and a magazine feed, which also led to the development of machine-guns. The breech-loader did not come into its own until the 1880s.

Whereas in 1815 a musket was accurate to about 100 yards (although it had a killing range of about 200 yards), by the early-1860s this had increased to about 500 yards, and by 1900 was greater than 1000. Artillery range comparably rose from about 1,000 yards in 1815 to 3,000 in the early 1860s and then 6,500 by 1900. The rate of change also rose with many inventions, such as recoil and recuperator systems for artillery which increased its accuracy (1872), smokeless propellants which cut the smoke blocking accurate aiming (1884) and quick-locking breech mechanisms for artillery (1880s).

The net effect, for both hand-held firearms and artillery, was substantial changes in precision, mobility and speed of use. Commanders faced the problem of how best to respond as, due to defensive firepower, massed frontal attacks on prepared positions became more costly. The result was a move, first, away from close-packed units, not least with an emphasis on the skirmishing line, as with the Prussians in their successful wars with Austria (1866) and France (1870–1), and, second, towards the digging of entrenchments to provide cover, most prominently in the First World War (1914–18), but already seen in the closing stages of the American Civil War in Virginia.

There was also a marked change in the participants in warfare, one that brought together state formation and nationalism. This change was seen, most prominently for military historians, in the German Wars of Unification (1864–71), Prussia's wars with Denmark, Austria and France that remade the European system, with a strong Germany taking the central place. In practice, the change in participants was more long term. In the Mediterranean, for example, it was a case of France or Spain pursuing advantages, not, as earlier, Marseille/Provence or Barcelona/Catalonia. This was a shift dramatized when Louis XIV of France sent troops into Marseille in 1658, while the forces of Philip V of Spain successfully besieged Barcelona in 1714.

The process, however, was also problematic, with empires seeking to resist nationalism or what could be seen as proto-nationalism.

This resistance was particularly the case in what became Italy, with Austria, which ruled much of it, including Milan and Venice, opposing nationalism. Thus, in 1821, Austrian regulars, suppressing a rebellion against an ally, defeated untrained and poorly disciplined Neapolitan *carbonari* at Rieti and went on to occupy Naples, while in 1849 starvation and cholera led a rebellious Venice to surrender to blockading Austrians. In 1859, however, the Austrians were defeated by a combination of French and Piedmontese troops, while in 1860 an Italian volunteer force under Giuseppe Garibaldi took southern Italy from the Neapolitan Bourbons in one of the most complete victories of the period 1816–1913. This conquest was the major step in the *Risorgimento* (unification of Italy), a movement for which the revolutionary Garibaldi was the military totem, although much of the work was done by the regulars of the Piedmontese army, especially, but not only, in 1859.

The ending of the old order was even more clearly demonstrated in 1870, when the Papal States were successfully invaded by the new Italian army. The French forces that had been able to restore Papal authority in 1849, overthrowing the Roman Republic, were, instead, committed to an unsuccessful war with Prussia. In 1849, these French troops had been brought by steamship and rail, an instance (as with the British support for the Ottomans against Russian pressure) of the process by which the old Mediterranean order had become reliant on the support of 'modern' forces.

European empires were successful in expanding outside Europe, but the military environment was different there. In contrast to Europe, the earlier formations of line, column and square remained more important in imperial conflict in the late nineteenth century. In part, this deployment was in order to accentuate Western firepower, in part because non-Western opponents were generally unable to produce a comparable hail of fire, and in part because Britain, the most active imperial power, lacked direct experience of European warfare between the Crimean War with Russia (1854–6) and the First World War.

This tactical conservatism did not stop the conquest of most of Africa (as well as much else) between 1870 and 1905, but it exposed European forces to serious problems when they encountered well-armed and well-led forces, as with the Italian defeat by the Ethiopians at Adua (Adowa) in 1896, the British defeats at the hands of the Afrikaner Boers in southern Africa in 1881 and 1899–1900 and those of Russia by the Japanese in Manchuria in 1904–5. Yet, the situation was more complex because these defeats in part reflected the ability and willingness of opponents to adopt Western techniques and technology, and to gain access to Western weaponry, as the Ethiopians did from the French. Moreover, the British eventually defeated the Boers in 1900–2, just as, after initial setbacks, especially the early stages of the siege of Plevna, the Russians had defeated the Turks in 1878. The Ethiopians were to be conquered by Italy in 1935–6; and the Japanese by the Soviet Union in 1945, in one of the most rapid and decisive campaigns of the Second World War, albeit one achieved at the expense of an already seriously weakened power.

The British were helped by the extent to which transoceanic operations were enhanced by technology in the shape of steamships, trains, telegraphy and improved medicines. In turn, these and other developments reflected the combination of applied knowledge, organizational skills and expenditure. Yet, these advantages had to be refracted through the nature of the military and physical environments, which ensured a variety of challenges. Thus, in southern Africa, the bush and forest that covered much of their lands enabled the Xhosa to stage a lengthy guerrilla resistance to the British, while the open veldt of Zululand encouraged the Zulus to pitched battles in 1879 in which, after an initial success, they were destroyed by British firepower. Colonial campaigning saw advances in the use of firepower as with the first use of the rifle grenade: by Spanish troops in Morocco in 1909.

Imperial expansion by European powers led to competition between them. Thus, in the Crimean War (1854–6), Britain and France came to the assistance of the Ottomans in order to prevent

Russia from dominating the Black Sea and the Balkans. The Russian navy was capable of beating the Ottomans at Sinope in 1853, but was not willing to engage with the British navy. Suspicion of Russian designs in 1878, when the Russian army advanced to within 15 kilometres of Constantinople, led the British to take a protectorate over Cyprus, thus gaining a base in the eastern Mediterranean, and to prepare to resist any Russian naval move through the Dardanelles. Concern about both Russian and French ambitions, and fear about a threat to the route to India, led the British to move into Egypt in 1882. The latter was of greater strategic importance with the opening, in 1869, of the Suez Canal which greatly shortened the route. Thus, strategy was linked to economics.

Resources, notably, but not only, in the shape of industrial capacity were important in capability and warfare. This was clearly seen in the American Civil War (1861–5), and at sea even more than on land. Enjoying a far greater capacity to launch, equip and man warships, the Union (North) was able to blockade the Confederacy (South), gravely handicapping its economy by cutting its trade links. Union amphibious attacks were important, not least in the seizure of New Orleans, the Confederacy's largest city, in 1862, and in subsequent operations on the Mississippi River in 1863 which cut the Confederacy in half. On land, the Confederacy was put under great pressure in the early stages, but its main field army, the Army of Northern Virginia under Robert E. Lee, regained the initiative in the summer of 1862 and mounted invasions of Union states in 1862 and 1863.

These invasions, however, came to an end with the Battles of Antietam and Gettysburg respectively, and thereafter the initiative overwhelmingly lay with the Union, creating a sense of inexorable pressure in which resources played a major role. For long unsuccessful on the Eastern front, Union forces to the west, after their success in the Mississippi Valley, were able to clear eastern Tennessee and advance on Atlanta. Having seized that in 1864, their army, under William Tecumseh Sherman, marched overland through Georgia to the Atlantic, wreaking damage and exposing the inability of Confederate forces to protect their heartland. By then, the new Union commander in the east, Ulysses S. Grant, was, starting with the Overland campaign, employing continual attacks to wear down the Confederate forces in Virginia, albeit at the cost of attritional tactics.

When he surrendered in 1865, Lee told his men they had been defeated by superior resources. The Union certainly had the advantage in manpower, tax receipts, industrial and agricultural production, trade, railway mileage, shipping and bullion. Yet, it was also important that Union forces had become more effective, not least due to the combination of experience and the application of organizational advantages in communications and logistics. The movement and supply of such numbers of men was unprecedented in North America. The maintenance of political determination was also significant, as there were many politicians willing to consider a partial accommodation of the Confederacy in order to end the war.

This factor helps explain Confederate strategy. It was impossible for their forces to conquer the Union, but, by attacking and winning battles, it seemed viable to hope that war-weariness there could be encouraged, while also dealing with the logistical problems of resting on the defensive. The possibility of Abraham Lincoln, the Union President, failing to win re-election in 1864 was especially important, and Lincoln was convinced that war news, particularly that of the fall of Atlanta to Sherman, was crucial to the election campaign.

This political dimension can be forgotten if attention focuses on weapons and battles, but it is all-important not least in explaining the determination of Western states to build up their armies and navies in the late nineteenth and early twentieth centuries in a competitive race that included the negotiation of alliances and the extension of conscription. The political dimension was also central in the use of armies to maintain civil order. Thus, in 1898, workers' protests in Milan led to a riot in which troops fired on an unarmed crowd, causing heavy casualties. The general responsible, Bava Beccaris, was given a special medal by Umberto I of Italy for the 'great service . . . rendered to our institutions and to civilization'.

A high level of military preparedness in Europe, a preparedness of planning as well as forces, contributed to the crisis that led to the outbreak of the First World War in 1914, as it made it more dangerous not to match the mobilization of possible rivals. Indeed, the prospect of waiting to be attacked by the forces that could be deployed was sufficiently hazardous to encourage mounting the first attack, a situation that looked towards planning for nuclear conflict during the Cold War. This situation helped ensure that, whereas the First (1912–3) and Second (1913) Balkan Wars between the local powers did not lead towards a more widespread conflict, the 1914 crisis involving Serbia and Austria provoked action or counter-action by all the major European powers. Russian pressure in 1914 on behalf of its Serbian protégé was accompanied by German mobilization on behalf of its Austrian ally, so as to be able to attack its rivals Russia and France. Moreover, the danger of war on two fronts helped lead to a German attack on Russia's ally France. This attack was designed to repeat the Prussian/German success of 1870, before polishing off Russia, which, it was thought, could only mobilize more slowly.

As the Germans advanced on Paris via Belgium from the flatter and more vulnerable north-east, rather than from the east, this brought Britain into the war as the guarantor of neutral Belgium. Focusing on military strategy and operational planning, the German General Staff, which like other commands underestimated the defensive potential of machine-gun and artillery fire (in part because they had not played a crucial role in the German Wars of Unification), had also devoted far too little attention to the politics of the war. The Germans mistakenly anticipated a quick victory before Britain could make much of a difference.

Later in the war, Italy (1915) and the United States (1917) joined in on the side of the Allies (Britain, France and Russia), while Turkey and Bulgaria allied with Germany and Austria. Germany lost the diplomatic struggle of alliance-building, with all the consequences for economic strength: the American economy was a crucial adjunct to that of Britain during the war. This assistance helped explain the importance of German submarine attacks on merchant shipping in the North Atlantic, although as in the Second World War, German submarine warfare was defeated by Allied resources, tactical and technological developments and organizational improvements.

If the pre-war international system helped explain the crisis of 1914, the nature of conflict over the previous decade was also indicative of what was to come. The Russo-Japanese War of 1904–5 had seen Japanese frontal attacks made very costly by the intensive defensive firepower provided by entrenched forces able to use machine guns and modern artillery. This was a war of front lines and barbed wire. Although not on the same scale, and not so intensively, the same was true of the Balkan Wars of 1912–3. Thus, Bulgarian attacks on the Turkish defensive lines to the west of Constantinople were beaten off with heavy losses as a result of firepower. Nevertheless, commentators were convinced from these conflicts that attacking forces with high morale would succeed. The racism of the period was such that it was argued that, if the Japanese could succeed, Europeans would readily succeed likewise, albeit at the cost of high losses. The First World War was to show otherwise.

Similarly, the naval dimension of the Russo-Japanese War was misleading as it centred on a decisive Japanese victory at Tsushima (1905), an engagement between battleships for which the results were even more complete and one-sided than Trafalgar had been. The Russian fleet had hoped to interrupt Japanese operations in East Asia. Instead, its total defeat helped to lead to the end of the war on Japanese terms and was seen as a Japanese victory. The battle was settled by long-range fire from battleships, while the naval dimensions of the conflict as a whole saw an extensive use of recent technology in the shape of torpedoes and mines. This situation looked towards the First World War, although submarines were not employed in the Russo-Japanese War. Nor, despite British hopes, was the First World War to see a decisive battle, let alone one comparable to Tsushima.

Another theme of partial continuity is that of conflict outside Europe. There were obvious contrasts between Western versus non-Western conflict in Africa prior to 1914 and that between Anglo-French and German forces there from 1914, but there were also shared problems in the shape of logistics. As a more obvious form of continuity, the war with Germany's ally Turkey was an echo of pre-1914 conflict, notably for Russia with Turkey but also as an instance of warfare with non-Western powers that were Westernizing or, at least, changing. Thus, Britain's defeats by the Turks (who displayed considerable combat effectiveness) at Gallipoli and at Kut (in modern Iraq) in 1915 can be seen as another instance comparable to Italy's defeat by Ethiopia at Adua in 1896, while the final British success achieved in 1918, with the conquest of Iraq, Palestine and Syria, was another stage of the process of defeating non-European states, a process seen with China, Persia and Turkey over the previous 70 years.

This continuity is important for there is a tendency to see the First World War in terms of novelty, not least with regard to scale and character but also with respect to weapons either completely new, especially tanks and gas, or on a far greater scale, particularly submarines and aircraft. This novelty encourages discussion in terms of modern and total war and clearly the scale was very different from wars within Europe over the previous 90 years. There was certainly no comparison with the Anglo-French war with Russia – the Crimean War – nor with the Austro-Prussian or Franco-Prussian Wars. The numbers of troops raised in the First World War were far greater than in any of these wars, as were the losses, or indeed the duration of the First World War. The largest fall in life expectancy since the Black Death of the fourteenth century may well have occurred in France during the First World War. A difference in scale was indeed an aspect of novelty, but that is not the same as some of the claims for novelty made on behalf of the war. Instead, it is valid to note continuity with elements of recent conflicts, not least the extent of trench warfare in the last year of the American Civil War in Virginia as well as the Russian siege of Turkish-held Plevna in 1878 and the Russo-Japanese War of 1904–5. Protracted trench warfare therefore was not an aberration, but a continuation of a trend towards immobility that had begun in the mid-nineteenth century. This was not merely due to the huge increases in firepower and the use of inappropriate tactics. At the heart of the problem was the illogical belief that defensive firepower could be overcome by élan, while trusting that offensive firepower could cause enough damage to the enemy to allow the assault to succeed. However, no one truly appreciated just how destructive the artillery and small arms of the early-twentieth century had become, the Russo-Japanese War notwithstanding, it took everyone by surprise.

At the same time, there were also important changes in methods of fighting during the war. The fluidity of operations on the Western Front in 1914, as the Germans advanced and the British and French counter-attacked in the First Battle of the Marne, stopping the Germans short of Paris, was followed by the more static nature of trench warfare there in 1915–7, and then by the opening up of the Western Front by both sides in 1918. That year, the Germans displayed tactical skill during their spring offensives, but not the ability to use this to operational and strategic effect. The offensives stuttered to a halt each time.

The German failure of understanding, goals and planning was not matched by the Allies (Britain, France and the United States). Their combined artillery-infantry tactics, and their ability to maintain the operational dynamic proved able to overcome German defensive strength, with the British proving particularly impressive with an all-arms army that represented a major improvement over the unskilled mass volunteer and conscript British armies of 1915–6. Similarly with the Americans. John Pershing, the commander of the American Expeditionary Force, who had insisted that his men train for 'open' instead of trench warfare, was soon disabused as a result of heavy American casualties. Open warfare did not return until the

Allied counter-offensive of late 1918, in which deep-battle tactics destroyed much of the German army. The skills of the German army at the time of the spring offensives were largely restricted to the élite stormtroopers and the rest of the army was less well trained. In contrast, the British developed specialist assault divisions but did not neglect the rest of the combat troops as far as new skills in all-arms tactics were concerned.

The ability to maintain the operational dynamic displayed by the Allies in 1918 looked towards the success of offensives in the Second World War, although the capability at the disposal of attacking forces was more effective in the Second World War as a consequence of the mobile artillery offered by the large-scale use of tanks. The Allies were also helped by their eventual victory in the air war. War planes developed greatly in numbers and sophistication during the course of the war and, by 1918, France was able to launch bombing raids of over 100 aircraft. Air superiority was also crucial in ensuring the detailed reconnaissance information that was vital for artillery and for more general planning, while denying such advantages to the enemy.

Aircraft, like tanks, attract a lot of attention, but the key killer was artillery. During the war, the number, strength, precision and use of artillery improved vastly. The French, for example, were very much helped in resisting the German offensive at Verdun in 1916, an attempt to force destructive attrition on the French, by an effective use of artillery, now heavier than their guns in 1914. This use included the creeping barrage, when gunfire falls just in front of advancing troops, which was employed to support the French counter-offensive at Verdun in October 1916. On 18 July 1918, the French counter-offensive on the Marne was supported by a creeping barrage, with one heavy shell per 1.27 yards of ground, and three field artillery shells per yard. In the face of such firepower, the numbers of infantry were the vital resource. For example, the number of British infantry divisions in France increased from five in August 1914 to 58 by the end of 1916. The economy was also directed and the home front mobilized, with British output of artillery shells, for example, rising from 500,000 in 1914 to 76.2 million in 1917. More positively, the application of new technology and state power helped ensure that the percentage of casualties arising from disease fell markedly in comparison with conflicts over the previous centuries. Whereas the ratio between death to disease and combat fatality had been 1.9 to 1 for the British in the Boer War (1899–1902), it was 0.67 to 1 for British and Dominion troops in the First World War, and 0.09 to 1 for the Second World War.

In considering the First World War, it is possible to focus on the stasis of the trenches, while the horrors of the fighting there dominates attention, but that focus overlooks the extent to which this stasis was partly overcome in 1918 by semi-mobile warfare, although the German line remained unbroken at the time of the Armistice. Nevertheless, Germany, one of the world's leading economies, and its allies, Austria, Bulgaria and Turkey, were defeated in roughly the same period of time as the Confederacy in the American Civil War. Moreover, the war had also witnessed a series of other defeats, most obviously of Russia, which was knocked out of the conflict in 1918 after the strains of war and defeat by Germany had helped lead to the overthrow in 1917 of first the monarchy and then the liberal republic that succeeded it.

The length of the struggle combined with the amount of resources used up by the large armies, notably shells for the military, helped ensure that the burden on society was heavy. This burden escalated social changes, notably with the greater participation of women in the workforce, large-scale inflation and a decline in social deference. The net effect was a strengthening of the Left politically, while obedience within empires was placed under pressure. This was particularly apparent in Central Asia, where resistance to conscription in the Russian army led to rebellion in 1916, and also in Ireland where there was a rising in Dublin the same year.

The aftermath of the First World War is usually treated in terms of the learning of lessons and moves towards the Second World War, which broke out, in Europe, in 1939. This is a reasonable approach in hindsight, but it ignores both the key problem of the victorious powers in the early 1920s – maintaining imperial control and influence – and the extent to which the major struggles of the period 1919–36 were civil wars in Russia and China. Western imperialism reached its territorial height in the aftermath of the 1919 peace settlement because, although Japan gained German-ruled Pacific islands, the Turkish Empire was partitioned, with Britain and France gaining key shares in terms of both territory and influence. This was the most important extension of Western power into the Arab and Turkish worlds hitherto, and one that brought millions of Muslims under Western control; in addition to those already under British rule in South Asia. Palestine and Trans-Jordan became British-mandated territories and Lebanon and Syria French ones.

However, there was massive resistance, in particular to British control of Iraq and Egypt, which Britain had gained control of in the share-out of the Turkish Empire, French rule of Syria and Spanish rule of northern Morocco. These problems were followed, in 1936–9, by the Arab rising in Palestine. The resistance indicated the difficulties facing Western imperialism as an incorporating form of power, and that there was no simple transfer from Turkish to Western imperial rule. Militarily, Western forces encountered some of the problems that were to be seen in the 2000s, notably with the difficulty of dealing with irregulars, of maintaining supply routes and of protecting supporters.

Success was mixed. Using local allies (Druze and Maronite Christians) and brutal force (aircraft and artillery bombing and bombarding the city of Damascus), the French suppressed opposition in Syria in 1925–6, while, after initial Spanish defeats, French and Spanish forces, using air-dropped gas (and also the first amphibious landing by tanks), enforced control in Morocco. The British, their empire under considerable strain as a result of overstretch, had less success, and had to abandon interests and pretensions to power in Egypt, Iraq and Persia.

The most serious Western defeat, however, was that of the Greek intervention in Turkey, as Greece, a member of the wartime Allied coalition, strove to ensure its war gains from Turkey. As an aspect of a more general trend in much twentieth-century conflict, Turkish success was followed by the 'ethnic cleansing' of Greeks from communities on the Aegean coast where they had lived for thousands of years. Moreover, this success proved the basis for a bellicose nationalism focused on the war-leader, and first President, Ataturk, and on the Turkish army.

If the Middle East proved a tough haul for the victorious powers, Russia proved a goal too far. Forces from the major powers, notably Britain, France, Japan and the USA, had intervened in Russia. Initially this was to prop up Russia as an ally against Germany and to prevent Allied *matériel* from falling into German hands. Subsequently, intervention was designed to help the 'Whites' (anti-Communists) against the Communists in the post-war Russian Civil War, but, though successful on specific fronts, the Whites proved seriously divided and unable to mount a coherent challenge. Western forces, provided by a reluctant public, proved no substitute. Benefiting, moreover, from control over the central points of the transport and industrial system (Moscow and St Petersburg) and from their ability to seize resources, the Communists had a more disciplined response.

The fighting lacked the density of force seen in the First World War and was much more fluid than that had been, a point also true of the civil warfare in China in the 1920 and 1930s by the warlords, the Kuomintang (Nationalists) and the Communists. This contrast serves as a reminder of the range of conflict that military commentators had to consider. Similarly, warfare in Latin America, especially the (very different) civil wars of the Mexican Revolution (1911–6) and the Chaco War between Bolivia and Paraguay (1932–5), were characterized by a relatively low force density combined with the serious problems posed by logistical deficiencies that reflected the primitive nature of communications as well as the limited resources of these poor economies.

It was against this background that governments responded to commentators who claimed that the future lay with airpower or tanks. These arguments attracted considerable attention and were not without effect. Thus, the British air force, the newly established, independent Royal Air Force, was employed to try to maintain control of colonies, offering an alternative to the mobile column of troops. The reality on the ground, however, was generally limited, with bombing, for example of the strongholds of the 'Mad Mullah' in Somaliland (part of modern Somalia) in 1920, having only a small impact.

The theorists did not, however, focus on counter-insurgency warfare. Instead, they argued that new technology ensured that, in the event of another conflict between major states, it would be possible to achieve victory more rapidly and at less cost than in the First World War, a goal that the trauma of heavy casualties in that conflict made necessary. Moreover, given that it was assumed that opponents would be investing in such technology (as had happened in that conflict), it would be necessary to use this weaponry more effectively. In some respects, the language employed was akin to that of the Revolution in Military Affairs in the 1990s (see pp. 72, 155), and this testified to the strong commitment to change and success through change that is a characteristic, indeed in many respects *the* defining characteristic, of modern warfare. Key figures included Douhet, Mitchell and Trenchard for air power, and Fuller and Liddell Hart for tanks. Mitchell, for example, argued in 1921 that the first battles of any future war would be air battles and that they offered the potential for decisive victory. In 1923, he pressed for an American alliance with Canada in order to be able to bomb Japan into defeat in any future war.

Yet governments faced with the crushing fiscal overhang from the First World War and the extent of current non-military commitments were wary of such ideas for a transformation in military capability, doctrine and planning; while military establishments confronting the range of imperial obligations were wary of investing too heavily in any one sector. For Britain and France, with their colonial garrisons and conflicts, as well as their navies, there was only so much that could be spent on high-spectrum air and land weaponry. There was also a need for the availability of troops able to maintain order at home, as in Britain with the General Strike in 1926. This aspect of military commitment tends to be underplayed, but it was important, as in the United States in 1932 when troops were used to drive the Bonus Army from Washington because the demonstrators were seen as subversive. Conversely, in some countries, the military took part in seizures of power. In Portugal, where Sidónio Pais, a general, seized power in 1916, being shot by a veteran the following year, there were over 20 attempted coups between 1910 and 1926, when a successful coup was staged by a group of conservative army officers, headed by José Mendes Cabeçadas.

British and French choices for force structure were not essentially a matter of conservatism, but the consequences appeared such, not least in comparison with militaries that seemed more flexible in part because of a more restricted range of commitments. This latter situation was true of both Germany and the Soviet Union (Communist Russia), each of which had to rebuild their militaries: the first when post-war disarmament was rejected by Adolf Hitler after he gained power in Germany in 1933, and the second as a new military was created from the crucible of the Russian Civil War. Moreover, in both states there was an ideology of the new. This ideology proved particularly receptive to new weaponry and to novel ideas of how best to use it. In the Soviet Union, after debate in the 1920s about the extent to which peoples' warfare or regular military institutions should be preferred, there was interest in the 1930s in the idea of the operational scale of war, that between tactics and strategy, as well as in large tank forces. These ideas, however, were cut short as a result of the devastation inflicted by the large-scale purges of the late 1930s, as Josef Stalin, the Soviet dictator, turned on the military leadership and officer corps which he regarded as harbouring disloyalty. These purges greatly affected Soviet military effectiveness, certainly into 1942, and provide a prime example of the impact of politics on military developments.

In contrast, there was no serious falling out between the German military leadership and Hitler prior to 1944, when the leadership was purged after an attempt to kill Hitler and stage a coup, the July Bomb Plot. Instead, there was a unity of purpose, with the military happy to see an authoritarian dictatorship pouring resources into a major build-up. Hitler also supported a modernization focused on mechanization and air power. German commanders took forward 1920s' German and British theories of armoured warfare and developed panzer divisions to give force to them. German warmaking was to prove effective in 1939–41, but that led to a lack of attention to weaker German fundamentals, not least the failure to relate moves to a sensible wider strategy or to build up an adequate military-industrial capability, both aspects of Hitler's fatal overconfidence. These flaws were to become readily apparent in 1941–45, but, prior to the war, Germany appeared, especially to its leadership, to represent the future of warfare. The use of German planes to launch a devastating air attack on the town of Guernica during the Spanish Civil War 1936–9 suggested that this future would be one in which civilians would be in the front line, which had been only occasionally the case during the First World War, although the Germans had bombed London then. Indeed, air power theorists justifying the existence of air forces argued that civilian populations could be deliberately targeted in order to break the will to fight and thus overcome the tactical impasse on the front line. This strategy was seen as a way of ensuring a quick war, and, in particular, of avoiding a repetition of the First World War. The Spanish Civil War also suggested that planes might serve as a substitute for artillery. Yet, despite the emphasis by outside commentators on air power, the Spanish Civil War was overwhelmingly an infantry struggle.

At the same time, a war to which insufficient attention was de-voted by Western contemporaries suggested that aggressive policies and the strategic and operational offensive might not deliver the anticipated results, a key instance of the contrast between output and outcome. Having, in 1931–2, attacked and conquered the Chinese province of Manchuria, the leading industrial region in China, Japan had pressed on to launch a full-scale conquest of China in 1937, which really marked the beginning of the Second World War. The Japanese were successful in seizing the major Chinese cities – Beijing, Shanghai and, followed by a terrible massacre, Nanjing in 1937, and Canton in 1938, as well as inflicting major blows on Chinese forces – but were unsuccessful in forcing China to surrender. Instead, the Japanese found that they had taken on an intractable struggle that involved high costs and the commitment of much of their resources, a reprise of what threatened to be their situation in the Russo-Japanese War. Because the latter was marginal to the centres of Russian power, it had proved possible for Nicholas II to accept failure and to bring the war to a close, but that outcome was not possible for the Kuomintang leader, Chiang Kai-Shek. The Japanese goal – a number of client regimes in a divided China – was advanced without any real sense of how it was to be achieved: as so often with war, there was a mismatch between goal and process, with the latter, moreover, largely conceived only in military terms.

Japanese failure (in victory) in China helped lead to the outbreak of war in the Pacific, as it led Japan, in 1941, to seek both resources for its China policy and non-interference with this policy by other powers. This decision resulted in the seizure of the colonies of the European states weakened by war in Europe (Britain, the Dutch and France) – Hong Kong, Malaya, British Borneo, the Dutch East Indies (now Indonesia), Burma and Indo-China (Vietnam/Cambodia/Laos) – and also in attack on the United States, the power best placed to oppose this seizure and to contest Japan's China policy.

At the same time, Japanese failure in China anticipated that of Hitler. It proved possible for Germany to defeat and conquer Poland (1939), Denmark, Norway, the Netherlands, Belgium and France (1940), Yugoslavia, Greece and large areas of the Soviet Union (1941), but it was not possible to ground the new empire in popular support, nor to persuade Britain to end resistance, nor to define the basis for a settlement with the Soviet Union, nor to win much effective backing in conquered areas for Germany's conflict with Britain and the Soviet Union. This multiple failure was more important than the tactical and operational successes best summarized as *Blitzkrieg* because this failure helped to ensure a weakness that could be exploited from 1942 by the superior resources and, eventually, much improved fighting effectiveness of Germany's opponents, especially Britain, the United States and the Soviet Union.

Without suggesting any similarities in methods, there was a parallel with the failure to ground Anglo-French imperial rule in the Middle East in the 1920s, but this rule did not face external opponents equivalent to those directed against Germany and Japan in the early 1940s. At the same time, this argument can only be pushed so far, for, just as the British and French empires won support, Germany's allies included Bulgaria, Finland, Hungary, Italy and Romania, as well as a considerable degree of support from new states created by Hitler (Croatia, Slovakia, Vichy France) and from other interested parties.

To probe another difference with the British and French empires, Hitler was ideologically and (like Napoleon) psychologically committed to continual conflict. Empire, for him and his supporters, was a means to a meta-historical goal of racial superiority, especially over Slavs, and the slaughter of all Jews, as well as a new world order. This German-directed racial new world, however, was not an outcome possible without a total victory on the pattern of the pyramids of skulls left by medieval Asian conquerors when punishing opposition. Many of Hitler's generals proved willing to disregard international law and common decency in framing and executing criminal measures, for example allowing the slaughter of Jews as well as the treatment of Soviet prisoners such that large numbers died.

The outcome Hitler sought was beyond his grasp once he had added war with the United States (December 1941) to his invasion of the Soviet Union (June 1941). The fate of the latter (Operation Barbarossa) cast light on the limitations of German warmaking. The initial successes of *Blitzkrieg* had relied not only on the weaponry and tactical adeptness of the German *Wehrmacht* (army) and *Luftwaffe* (air force), but also, as it turned out, on other factors. First, the German ability to fight sequential one-front campaigns, rather than face sustained large-scale conflict on more than one front (which did not occur until 1944), was crucial. Second, serious deficiencies in the planning of Germany's opponents were very important. Poland, Yugoslavia and Greece tried to defend long frontiers with strung-out forces, rather than concentrating reserves, Denmark and Norway were surprised, while France put its reserves in the wrong place and totally lost control of the tempo and flow of the campaign.

In the Soviet Union, however, there were important differences in 1941. The Soviets were able to organize defence in depth and reserves, which ensured that the *Wehrmacht*'s initial successes, with the heavy casualties inflicted on the Red Army, did not end the campaign. Moreover, important tactical, operational and strategic deficiencies in German warmaking were revealed. As far as the first was concerned, the inability of infantry and artillery to keep up with the advance of the German tanks exposed the latter to the problems of overcoming Soviet defensive positions, especially their anti-tank fire: the anti-tank gun was one of the most underrated weapons of the war. Operationally, there was confusion between German plans centred on capturing territory and those focused on destroying Soviet units. This confusion led to a lack of agreement over whether to advance on Moscow or to turn troops from this central axis south in order to overrun Ukraine and destroy the Soviet forces there (the option that was chosen). Strategically, insufficient thought had been devoted to translating successes into victory.

These problems ensured that the *Wehrmacht* had failed before a Soviet counter-offensive, launched on 5–6 December 1941 and mounted in bitter winter weather, drove the Germans back from Moscow. After considerable losses, the *Wehrmacht* blocked this counter-offensive, which had been mounted on too wide a front to sustain impetus.

In turn, in June 1942, Hitler launched Operation Blue. As a consequence of the *Wehrmacht's* losses and difficulties over the previous year, and the need to concentrate strength in order to achieve success, this offensive was mounted on only the southern half of the German front. As with Barbarossa, Blue suffered from inconsistent objectives. A drive to seize the oilfields in the Caucasus, and thus to deal with this acute resource problem, was confused with the goal of capturing a bridgehead over the River Volga at the city of Stalingrad. Strong resistance there ensured a stress on the value of destroying Soviet forces in an attritional fashion, as with the unsuccessful German advance against the French at Verdun in 1916. In practice the intractable nature of the devastated urban terrain, combined with the Soviet ability to resupply from the eastern bank of the river, thwarted the Germans in Stalingrad.

Thus, operational opportunities had been reduced to tactical impasse. This failure set the stage for a Soviet counter-offensive in December 1942 through weak-flanking Romanian units, so that the German Sixth Army in Stalingrad was surrounded. Hitler had refused permission to withdraw and attempts both at relief and at aerial resupply failed. The Soviets drove in the German position and the Sixth Army surrendered in February 1943.

Stalingrad, the crucial battle in stopping the German advance followed that of Midway (4 June 1942), which had been the key blow against further Japanese advances. Helped by surprise, and by superior fighting qualities on land, which reflected greater determination as well as the experience gained by conflict in China, the Japanese had mounted a series of successful assaults in the winter of 1941–2 on the Western position in South-East Asia and the Western Pacific. British forces in Malaya, Singapore and Burma, and the American army in the Philippines were all seriously outfought, and the Dutch East Indies were also overrun. The surrender of a large British army in Singapore in February 1942 to a smaller but better led Japanese force proved an especially acute humiliation. In addition, Japanese air power proved particularly effective against Allied warships.

Having created an extensive empire, the Japanese sought to strengthen it in the South-West and Central Pacific, but, after being checked by the American navy in the Battle of the Coral Sea, they were heavily defeated, on 4 June 1942, at Midway, a battle that led to the loss of four Japanese aircraft carriers to American carrier-based air attack. The Japanese defeat owed much to American command quality, to the American ability to seize advantage of unexpected opportunities and to the more general resilience of American naval capability. Midway demonstrated that battles at sea would now be dominated by air power rather than the exchanges between battle-ships seen at Tsushima (1905) and Jutland (1916).

Midway changed the arithmetic of air power, not least because the Americans proved much more able to replace trained pilots, while their superior air and naval construction systems produced more units than the Japanese. This paralleled the American contribution to the Battle of the Atlantic against German submarines, posing a strategic problem for the latter that interacted with the tactical and operational challenges offered by improved Allied proficiency in anti-submarine warfare, not least in the use of air support.

The Allied proficiency was a matter of superior resources, improved tactics and the use of scientific advances. The latter had already been seen in the development of radar, which was a prime example of the crucial contribution of scientific advances to the conduct of war. Radar's capacity for long-distance detection of movement was vital because of the greater range and speed of military units, which made reliance on human observers of less value. Radar sets were installed in British warships from 1938. It played an even more important role in helping the defence against German air attack in the Battle of Britain in 1940. This use was followed by the invention of the sophisticated cavity-magnetron which was central to the development of microwave radar.

The submarine war with Germany, won by the Allies in the second quarter of 1943, in part by the large-scale use of air cover against submarines, was the crucial prelude to the build-up of Allied strength in Britain preparatory to the invasion of German-occupied Western Europe. Launched on 6 June 1944, D-Day, this invasion, Operation Overlord, benefited not only from surprise but also from total air and sea dominance. The success of the initial landings was followed by a tough battle of consolidation and breakout in which the vulnerability of tanks to anti-tank fire was fully revealed, not least in repeated British failures to break through near Caen. The Battle for Normandy also showed one of the main values of air power: in tactical and operational support of land (as of sea operations). Thus, Allied air attacks proved heavily damaging to German tanks, while others helped hamper German routes to Normandy by focusing on bridges and rail links.

In contrast, there has been far greater controversy over the value of the strategic air war on Germany. This Combined Air Offensive very much brought German civilians into the front line, which was a key aspect of the extent to which this conflict pressed particularly hard on civil society. The air offensive on Germany has been criticized from different directions including the argument that the damage to German civilians and cities was immoral, indeed a war crime; and the very different claim that the air assault was not worth the cost both in Allied casualties and in the benefit foregone from the use of air power elsewhere. There has also been debate about the extent of the damage inflicted on the German economy and, in particular, on the military–industrial complex.

Conversely, it has been suggested that, but for this air assault, German production would have increased and that the air assault reduced the ability of the German economy to act in an integrated fashion and thus to benefit from modern manufacturing techniques. Such techniques were directly at issue in the production of German weaponry. For example, the MG-42 machine gun, introduced in 1942, was flexible, easy to use and could fire 1,200 rounds per minute. Easy to make, from mass-produced pressed steel parts, and inexpensive, this was the kind of *matériel* that posed a real challenge to advancing Allied forces. Attacks on German rail links and on the production of synthetic oil were especially important to the disruption of the German war economy. The heavy losses inflicted by the German military make it understandable that the Allies used the forces at their disposal, and it is somewhat anachronistic to condemn bombing for lacking the precision that was subsequently to be available. More specifically, the aircraft employed in the defence of Germany against air assault were not available for operations elsewhere, while close to a third of German artillery production was devoted to anti-aircraft guns.

By the summer of 1944, Soviet attacks on the Eastern Front had wrecked enormous damage on the German army and had also driven it a long way back. The last major German offensive on the Eastern Front led to the Battle of Kursk (5–13 July 1943) in which German armoured attacks on well-prepared Soviet defences failed to achieve the anticipated breakthroughs. The standard Soviet T-34 tank had been upgraded and was used effectively at close range, where it matched up well with the new German Panther and Tiger tanks. As Soviet production of tanks was far greater than that of Germany, the Red Army could better afford to take losses, and Kursk shifted the situation in their favour. The subsequent Soviet offensives achieved more lasting success than the winter offensives of 1941–2 and 1942–3. After Kursk, the Soviet army drove the Germans from much of Ukraine. Soviet forces benefited from the plentiful weaponry flowing from mass production, as well as from effective training and unit cohesion and good operational doctrine.

In 1944, there were important Soviet advances across the entire front. In particular, in Operation Bagration, the German Army Group Centre was destroyed (with over half a million casualties) as the Soviets advanced from Belarus to central Poland. Further south, the Soviets broke into the Balkans, leading Romania and Bulgaria to change sides and the Germans to evacuate Greece, Albania and most of Yugoslavia.

Anglo-American forces that had invaded Italy in 1943 had not achieved comparable success because, although this invasion had precipitated Italy's change of side to the Allied camp, the rapid German response had forced the Allies into slow advances. The campaign in Italy exemplified the continued tactical and operational strength of the defence, as well as the extent to which tanks could have limited impact. Some of the trench warfare was similar to fighting in the First World War, which looked towards the situation in the Korean War in 1951–3 after the initial manoeuvrist stages in 1950 ended.

Having cleared Normandy in hard fighting in which the ability of their infantry, artillery and tanks to operate in an integrated fashion was demonstrated, British and American forces made rapid advances in France and Belgium in 1944. This advance, however, created major logistical problems, while, as the Germans rallied in more difficult terrain, from the polders of the Scheldt to the forested mountains of the Hunsrück and the Vosges, the Allies were stalled. An attempt to force a breakthrough on a narrow front, the Arnhem offensive that September, again showed the strength of the defence, with British airborne units unable to open up the front.

Conversely, a large-scale German counter-attack launched on 16 December, the Battle of the Bulge, designed to regain the initiative for Hitler by leading Britain and the United States to negotiate peace, failed to achieve more than a local breakthrough and was also flawed strategically. Faced with an eventually firm defensive, supported, once the skies cleared, by potent Allied air power, the Germans suffered from an inability to sustain their offensive, which was not helped by a lack of oil. This failure provided the background for the successful overthrow of Germany the following spring as Soviet, American and British forces advanced simultaneously, with the Soviets achieving the key advance from the River Oder to Berlin, leading Hitler to commit suicide on 30 April.

By the end of 1944, the situation was also parlous for Japan and, indeed, the government that had committed her to war with the United States in 1941 resigned in the summer of 1944 after the loss of the Pacific island of Saipan put Japan within the range of American air attack. The American counter-attack began in the winter of 1942–3 with a difficult campaign centred on the Pacific island of Guadalcanal. As with the Australians on New Guinea, the Americans became more adept in jungle combat, while they also benefited from the increased ability to win superiority at sea and in the air.

In 1943, this gain of the initiative was translated into a policy of island-hopping, with the Americans focusing on particular islands and bypassing Japanese garrisons elsewhere, for example at Rabaul. Simultaneous advances were mounted in the South-West Pacific – along the coast of New Guinea and against nearby islands, as well as in the Central Pacific, with an advance against the Marshall and Mariana Islands. These advances involved a duplication of effort, but the Americans could afford it, and the cumulative strain on the Japanese was acute. In 1944, the American advances converged on the Philippines, destroying much of the remaining Japanese navy in battles fought to ensure that the Americans could land and operate there, especially the Battle of Leyte Gulf of 23–6 October. The Japanese had built new carriers to replace those lost at Midway, but lacked sufficient trained pilots.

As a reminder of the range of the war, 1944 also saw a major Japanese offensive in China, Operation Ichigo, in which much of the south was overrun as the Japanese created an unbroken route from their positions in central China to Canton and Vietnam. Moreover, underlining the integrated nature of the war, this success lessened Japanese exposure to the damaging American submarine attacks, which were wrecking the operation of their imperial system: the Japanese proved much less successful in anti-submarine warfare than the Allies against the Germans in the Atlantic. Japanese advances also captured the Chinese air bases intended for the American air assault on Japan, which increased the pressure on the United States to seize island bases in the Pacific.

In 1945, first Germany and then Japan were overcome. Superior Allied resources played a role, not least in the two American atomic bombs dropped on Hiroshima and Nagasaki in August 1945. This hitherto unprecedented weapon dramatized the inability of the Japanese military to protect the country and also provided an acceptable way for the Japanese government to concede defeat without losing face. More mundanely, German and Japanese forces were heavily outnumbered in *matériel*, which was a direct result of superior Allied economic mobilization. By 1945, the Americans had 30 large carriers and 82 escort-carriers off the coast of Japan. Moreover, American submarines were imposing an effective blockade and the US Army Air Force was devastating Japanese cities through conventional bombing.

Yet it is also necessary to note the extent to which Axis forces were outfought by the Allies as the latter displayed superior tactical and operational expertise. This was true, for example, of Burma, where the British had been beaten and driven out in 1942. British units subsequently learned to operate successfully in the forest, in both defensive and offensive operations, and were able to hold Japanese attacks on the Indian frontier in 1944 and to reconquer Burma in 1945, capturing Mandalay on 19 March and Rangoon on 3 May. Similarly, the Americans became more effective in combat with both German and Japanese units. The Soviets benefited from the experience gained in driving the Germans back to Berlin when they rapidly conquered Manchuria from the Japanese in August 1945, a key step in Japan's collapse.

The Second World War was followed by three decades of war and acute crisis in East, South and South-West Asia and Africa, and by a sustained large-scale military confrontation in Europe. Two key narratives came together in explaining this tension, first the pressures relating to and resulting from the struggle to end the Western colonial empires and, second, the rivalry between Communist and anti-Communist powers, the theme of the Cold War. The former struggle followed on from the collapse of the Italian and Japanese overseas empires with defeat in the Second World War, and saw conflict in South-East Asia in the late 1940s and early 1950s, culminating, in 1954, in the collapse of the French empire there.

There was also (far less successful) military pressure on the British in Malaya, in the shape of a Communist insurgency.

These, and other, decolonization struggles were perceived within the context of the Cold War, one that was accentuated greatly by the most important war of the period, and one that remains important to the political shape of the modern world: the Communist triumph in the Chinese Civil War of 1946–9. As a reminder of the extent to which interpretations of military capability and war both change and are heavily bound up with politics, it was for long argued that Communist victory in this conflict reflected the popularity of the Communists with the peasantry and, conversely, the decadence of the Kuomintang (Nationalist) regime, and that this victory was therefore in essence a product of political progress. This analysis was a conspicuous instance of a more general process of the demilitarization of military history, one in which other factors, especially political progress or superior resources, were employed, generally in a deterministic fashion, in order to explain what occurred.

This unsatisfactory approach risks both providing a false clarity and also underplaying the extent to which key factors in conflict are much more significant. Thus, in the case of the Chinese Civil War, the Kuomintang was guilty of a fatal strategic over-extension, moving troops into Manchuria to garrison the province, and leaving their garrisons vulnerable to the ability of the Communists to gain the initiative there, and to surround and destroy the isolated garrisons. From this secure base, supported with *matériel* by the neighbouring Soviet Union, the Communists then advanced south, although their success in conquering the rest of China was not without some hard fighting.

By the close of 1949, China was a Communist state, the British had abandoned their colonies in South Asia (India, Pakistan, Sri Lanka and Burma), as well as Palestine, the Dutch had been driven by a large-scale insurrection into abandoning what became Indonesia, and the French, having conceded independence to Syria and Lebanon, were under great pressure in Vietnam, in part as a consequence of the Communist victory in China, and the resulting support for the Viet Minh. This situation was not the end of European empires, and continued major efforts to sustain their empires were to be made by Britain, France and Portugal, but a dramatic shift had occurred.

That this shift made Communism more powerful, increased American disquiet and led to a major commitment of American resources, both to restrain Communism in Europe and also to resist its advances elsewhere. Thus, having sent aid in the late 1940s to resist Communist insurgents in Greece and the Philippines and to support Turkey against the Soviet Union, America played a key role in the establishment in 1949 of NATO (the North Atlantic Treaty Organization), a collective security system for protecting Western Europe from the Soviet advance. Crucially, this commitment was linked to the maintenance of a large American force in West Germany until the end of the Cold War, a force that put the Americans in the front line of any future European war, unlike the situation after the First World War.

In 1950, the United States, under a United Nations mandate, also committed ground troops to drive back the Communist North Korean invaders of South Korea which had a conservative, authoritarian and pro-American government. This invasion was a far more serious challenge than the Communist guerrilla campaign in the South which had been put down by early 1950. American success against the invaders led subsequently to an invasion of North Korea, intended to lead to the unification of Korea that, in turn, provoked Chinese intervention and the only formal conflict between leading powers since 1945, although it was not a declared war for either the United States or China.

Having been driven back, the Americans fought the Chinese to a halt. The Korean War (1950–3) encouraged a major build-up of the American military, as well as a greater concern with East Asia that was to lead to American troops being committed in large numbers in the 1960s and early 1970s in an eventually forlorn effort to prevent the Communist North Vietnamese from conquering South Vietnam.

By 1950, therefore, a post-Second World War order of international crisis and war seemed clear. When the Soviet Union brought its development of the atom bomb to fruition in 1949, the United States lost the comfort and apparent security of nuclear monopoly, and the Cold War expanded into a more dangerous arithmetic of mass destruction as both the United States and the Soviet Union built up their nuclear forces. Moreover, wars between India and Pakistan, and between Israel and its Arab neighbours in 1947–9, highlighted the extent to which the withdrawal of European colonial control meant new drives and opportunities for war, and with fighting different in some respect from that typical of the recent World War. Across much of Africa, this situation was to become even more the case in subsequent decades.

To the Present, 1950–

Many of the trends of the period 1950–90 were already clear in the late 1940s, and their playing out has a sense of dread predictability. Although the British were militarily successful in Malaya, European forces found it troublesome to hold on to colonies, in part because they could no longer enjoy sufficient tactical and operational advantages and in part because, resting on the defensive, they suffered from the strategic unwillingness to accept that only partial control was possible. These military factors interacted with the breakdown of the ability of imperial powers to ensure the incorporation of native élites and peoples within their empires, and from a lack of support at home for continued imperial efforts. The last proved particularly significant in the case of Britain and France in the late 1950s and early 1960s.

Loss of political will and unwillingness to pay the requisite military price was different from the tactical and operational inability to maintain control, but both played a role. By the end of 1962, France had abandoned most of its empire, most critically pulling out of Algeria, and by the end of 1964 this was also true of Britain. In 1967, Britain abandoned Aden in the face of an intractable local revolution that had broken out in 1963. Four years later, British forces withdrew from Singapore. Its government overthrown by discontented junior army officers, Portugal abandoned its African empire in 1974–5, giving victory to insurgents in Angola, Mozambique and Guineau-Bissau. The death of the Spanish dictator Franco in 1976 was followed by withdrawal from the Spanish Sahara.

This collapse of the European empires threw attention on the role of the United States, but its failure, despite a major commitment of force, in the Vietnam War of the 1960s and early 1970s created the misleading impression that, irrespective of the problems of colonialism, Western militaries could not prevail over non-Western popular warfare. In some respects, this impression prefigured that created more recently by conflict in Iraq and Afghanistan. The Vietnam War was the last of a web of wars for hegemony in the eastern half of Eurasia fought over the previous 70 years. The most significant were the Russo-Japanese War (1904–5), the American-Japanese War of the Pacific (1941–5), the Chinese Civil War (1946–9), the Korean War (1950–3) and the Vietnam War where, in the early 1960s, the United States provided steadily more military support to South Vietnam as it sought to resist attack by the Communist North. American military advisors were rapidly replaced by combat units, and the American military presence eventually rose to over 600,000 strong. Although the Americans, using conventional operators, thwarted the large-scale Communist assault in 1968, the Tet Offensive, defeating it and causing heavy casualties, their inability to secure victory led to withdrawal in 1973.

In the key stages before political support in the United States for the Vietnam War crucially ebbed in 1968, the American military failed to define an effective strategy or operational method. Instead, resorting to a solely military solution to the conflict, one to be largely secured through technology, not least in the form of bombing, the military measured success by statistics, principally body counts. This strategy, however, failed to address the need for a response that was more aware of military circumstances and political possibilities. The latter failure, however, was as much due to the multiple weaknesses of the South Vietnamese government as to the deficiencies of the United States, a point relevant today in Afghanistan. Although the Americans could not win, they defeated the Tet Offensive, blocked the large-scale North Vietnamese Easter Offensive of 1972 and used air power to force the North to accept President Richard Nixon's terms for withdrawing American combat forces. However, after the Americans had withdrawn, and while the American government was weakened by post-Vietnam and post-Watergate problems, the final North Vietnamese offensive led to the overrunning of South Vietnam in 1975.

The impression of the strength of non-regular forces was taken further in 1979–88 when the Soviet Army, despite, like the Americans in Vietnam, using considerable air power, could not overcome opposition by Muslim irregulars in Afghanistan where it was propping up a Communist client government. The difficulties experienced by the American-armed Israeli military in its protracted attempts in the 1980s to impose control in southern Lebanon contributed to the same impression.

Alongside these failings, the prominence of conflict between non-Western powers was shown by the Iran–Iraq War of 1980–8, the most costly conflict (in casualties) of the decade, and one fought to an inconclusive draw. The three India–Pakistan Wars (1948–9, 1965 and 1971) were important examples of such conflict, as were the wars between China and first India and then Vietnam in 1962 and 1979 respectively.

Similarly, war became common within Third World countries as force was used to impose and challenge control and authority. Some of these conflicts interacted with the Cold War, for example those between conservatives and radicals in Nicaragua and El Salvador in the 1980s, while for others the relationship was more tenuous. Thus, the Biafran (or Nigerian) Civil War of 1967–70 was largely due to the separatist drive of the Ibo of eastern Nigeria in opposition to what they saw as a northern/Muslim-run Nigeria.

The military also played a role in some First World countries, notably authoritarian regimes such as Spain, where the dictator, Franco, promoted himself to the rank of Captain General, a rank normally reserved for the sovereign, and Portugal where the 1958 presidential election saw the regime back Admiral Américo Tomás and thwart the opposition candidate General Humberto Delgado, as well as Greece where the military seized power in 1967. The Communist regimes of Eastern Europe also rested on force, a process demonstrated when liberal Communist regimes were overthrown by invading Soviet forces in Hungary in 1956 and Czechoslovakia in 1968. Force also played a role in the internal politics of democratic states, as with attempted coups, such as in Spain in 1981, planned coups, as in Italy in 1970, and terrorism, for example in Italy from 1969.

The lack of war or, rather, the wars that do not happen, are frequently a key element in military history, and this was certainly true of 1950–90. The United States and the Soviet Union came close to full-scale war, for example in 1962 (the Cuban Missile Crisis) and in 1983, but full-scale wars did not break out and the two powers only fought through surrogates, as in the Angolan Civil War of the late 1970s to early 1990s. The Arab–Israeli struggle also entailed an important element of great-power confrontation. This element was true not only of arms supplies (with Soviet-supplied MiGs competing in the air against American-supplied Phantoms), but also of planning. Soviet officers played a major role in the planning of Operation Granite, the surprise Egyptian attack on Israel in 1973 that launched the Yom Kippur War. Initially successful, this attack exposed the deficiencies of Israel's reliance on air and tank attacks in the absence of combined-arms operations. Israeli planes proved vulnerable to Soviet-supplied anti-aircraft weapons, but, once the Egyptians had advanced beyond this cover, they proved vulnerable and the Israelis successfully counterattacked, going on to advance across the Suez Canal and to force Egypt to peace.

Crucially, wars between surrogates did not escalate to involve the great powers directly, although this appeared a prospect at times, notably over the Middle East in 1967 and 1973. More generally, the large American and Soviet nuclear arsenals were not used during the Cold War. Moreover, Communist control in Eastern Europe and then the Soviet Union collapsed in 1989–91 with scant fighting and without the United States or NATO using their forces. Instead, internal problems and pressures within the Communist bloc, as well as the play of political circumstances, notably the policies of Mikhail Gorbachev, the Soviet leader from 1985, proved crucial. Conversely, greater determination and vigour on the part of Russian leaders in the late 2000s, combined with a bellicose military newly resurgent due to oil wealth, made Russia more unpredictable and, as Georgia discovered in 2008, a threat to its neighbours.

The combination of nuclear arsenals and the end of the Cold War led to talk of the obsolescence of war, but this was far from the case. Indeed, the 1990s saw a major conventional war between Iraq and an American-led coalition as Iraq, having invaded Kuwait in 1990, was driven out with heavy losses the following year. There was also sustained conflict in Central Africa, especially in Rwanda, Burundi and Congo. The ethnic violence this entailed led to large-scale massacres, notably in Rwanda in 1994, which dwarfed in scale, but matched in hatred, the killings linked to 'ethnic cleansing' in the former Yugoslavia in south-east Europe in the 1990s. There, fighting in Bosnia and Kosovo led eventually to international intervention by NATO forces, with these forces restricting themselves in combat to the use of air power.

This use of aircraft and cruise missiles encouraged confidence in the enhanced effectiveness of air superiority, which contributed to discussion of the supposed Revolution in Military Affairs (RMA). This effectiveness, however, was exaggerated, in part as a result of the contrast between output and outcome: the willingness of the Serbs to back down in Bosnia in 1995 in fact appears to have owed more to the success of Croat and Muslim forces on the ground, while in Kosovo in 1999 this decision may have been due to fears of a NATO land attack. In both cases, the unwillingness and inability of Russia to support Serbia was also an important element.

The idea that war had come to an end was already clearly redundant before the al-Qaeda attacks on New York and Washington in 2001 announced the War of Terror that the United States would try to counter with its War on Terror. The new American policy, however, faced many problems because terrorists do not provide a clear-cut target to match that of a conventional state. Partly as a result, the United States focused on surrogates linked to terrorism, first, in 2001, the Taliban regime in Afghanistan which had given the al-Qaeda leaders shelter, and, second, in 2003, Saddam Hussein of Iraq, whose policies, goals and rhetoric were seen as helping to destabilize the Middle East and certainly challenged American assumptions.

In each case, there was a rapid conquest, but it proved difficult to stabilize either country. American technological superiority, resources and training were important in leading to the rapid overthrow of Taliban and Iraqi forces, but guerrilla warfare and terrorist attacks challenged the sense of political control. This situation indicated the limitations of conventional forces and warmaking, and the need to match military commitments to a political strategy for resolution. Looked at from the other perspective, the terrorists and insurgents also found it difficult to achieve their military objectives.

Yet, by 2008, the Taliban resurgence in Afghanistan that had gathered pace from 2006 indicated the extent to which it was possible not only to undermine internal peace and order (the situation in much of Iraq), but also to thwart the process of government and repeatedly to challenge Western forces in combat. The problems Israel encountered when it attacked Hizbullah bases in southern Lebanon in 2006 were also indicative of the difficulties facing Western forces, both tactically and in terms of translating strength into a successful outcome. The same was true of Israeli problems in confronting the opposition of the *Intifada*, rebellion in occupied territories in Palestine that began in 1987 and, again, in 2000.

Without suggesting any political equivalence, other states seeking to suppress insurgencies also faced many difficulties. There were differences between Sudan, Sri Lanka, Burma and Congo, where insurgent groups controlled territory, and India, where, in Kashmir, it was more a case of terrorism, but the net impression was of the limitations of counter-insurgency. Yet, there were also successes in limiting insurgencies, for example in Colombia in the mid 2000s. The contrasting degree of success underlined the centrality of the political dimension, and thus the importance of aligning military with political strategies. In some countries, however, such as Afghanistan, these strategies faced the problems of the rise of warlordism in the context of failed states. There were, therefore, echoes of earlier forms of politics and warfare, echoes that represented major problems for those intervening in order to ensure and maintain the peace and to (re)build states.

A focus on insurrectionary and counter-insurrectionary warfare can lead to a lack of attention to the prospect that future warfare may involve confrontation or conflict between regular forces. Indeed, most military investment is for just such a capability, and notably so in east and south-east Asia. Moreover, much discussion and planning is for this type of conflict, for example between Israel and Iran or the United States and China. The variety of modern challenges and warfare, and the range of future prospects, underline the extent to which the nature of developments is unclear. However, it seems safe to predict that talk of the end of war and a peaceful future is highly unrealistic.

Conclusions: Assessing War

The centrality of war in history emerges clearly in any discussion of particular countries or of specific centuries. A brief study written by a British author for a British publisher risks putting the premium on conflicts involving Britain, but the emphasis here has been more wide-ranging, not least with the discussion of developments in China. Such a focus serves as a reminder of the very different political and geographical environments for conflict. A stress on contrasting political environments is of particular importance because there is a tendency to emphasize regular warfare – wars between states; rather than paying due attention to conflicts within states, such as, in the case of China, the Sanfen and Taipeng Rebellions and the Chinese Civil War.

An awareness of variety in goals, contexts and means of waging war underlines the difficulty of judging capability and assessing developments. The conceptualization of war and of military history is a sparse field. This might appear a surprising remark given the number of words deployed about Clausewitz, Jomini, [Sun Tzu], Mahan, Corbett and others, but is in fact the case. First, in comparative terms. The writing on the theory of social, gender or cultural history, for example, is far more extensive. Second, although particular writers, themes and episodes in military affairs and history have attracted conceptual literature, many have not. Moreover, the conceptualization has frequently been fairly simple. Whiggish notions of improvement in terms of a clear teleology are rampant, not least with regard to weapons technology. War and Society approaches also attracted teleological treatment, not least with the idea of improved social mobilization in modern industrial warfare. Alongside teleology came determinism, notably with the assumption that superior resources explained results. Thus, determinism was bound up with the material-culture approach to war.

A contrary approach, albeit one related in its simplicity, was the notion of national or cultural ways of war. This was an approach that drew on a number of roots, but particularly on the organic ideas of identity that became more prominent in the nineteenth century, which was very much an age influenced by biological approaches and, notably, Darwinian ideas of competition. These organic ideas of a distinctive response to environmental circumstances creating a synergetical basis for identity proved particularly interesting for those concerned with international competition. They led, moreover, to vitalist notions in which environment was linked to will. The concept of a national will proved especially conductive to commentators, not least those considering the nature of capability in an age of mass-conscript armies. The idea of superior national will appeared to provide an explanation for how to ensure success, particularly through better morale.

A separate strand contributing to the same end emerged from the idea of cultural competition. The concept of distinctive cultures appeared to match that of different national identities. Each drew on a notion of essentialism and one that can be seen as indicative of the strength of neo-Platonic ideas. Cultural essentialism was potent in the nineteenth century as a description both of present and past. It appeared to provide an explanation for Western expansion and also to link it with past conflicts that could be seen in cultural terms. The key rivalry was that of civilization and barbarism, and, to that, all else could be subordinated. This idea drew on the attractive notion that the then modern West was the embodiment of the Classical world. This linkage between Classical Greece and Rome and the modern Europe and the United States seemed obvious to commentators reading the classics in the original and seeing their legislators emerge from neo-Classical buildings. If the neo-Gothic Palace of Westminster did not appear to match this, nineteenth-century British prime ministers such as Derby and Gladstone not only read the classics in the original Greek and Latin, but also wrote knowledgeably about them.

The idea of a linkage was scarcely new at that juncture. While important during the Middle Ages, this idea had received a powerful boost from the Classical revival that had been so significant during the Renaissance. This revival had a direct military manifestation with interest in writers such as Machiavelli seeking to employ Classical ideas and models, a practice taken forward by the Princes of Orange during what was later seen as the Military Revolution of 1560–1660, and again by Maurice of Saxe and French commentators in the early eighteenth century. The sense of parallelism had varied manifestations over the following century, ranging from the response to Edward Gibbon's *Decline and Fall of the Roman Empire* (1776–88), a response that indicated a sense that Britain in the age of the American Revolution was moving in the same direction, to the conscious use of Classical echoes by the French Revolutionaries and Napoleon. Indeed, the latter was a modern Caesar, with his coup, his legions and his imperial aspirations.

Western imperialism during the post-Napoleonic century took this cultural approach to new heights. It drew on a revived *Romanitas*, with modern Western proconsular generals and governors seeing themselves as successors of the Romans. Napier's 'Peccavi', the Latin for 'I have sinned', in response to his conquest of the region of Sind in modern Pakistan in 1843 was commentary as much as joke: the magazine *Punch* portrayed him sending this telegram; in fact he never did so. Here, however, was another view of the modern Caesar, not as a Napoleon making war on fellow Europeans, but as a warrior bringing barbarians to heel. This idea also drew on a strong notion of religious superiority, and, in particular, on an activist pulse that was also seen in large-scale missionary activity.

The amalgamation of these ideas was important because war was waged outside Europe not only with those who could be presented as barbarians (not least by the application of a stadial [stages] theory of development), but also because there was conflict with states that were seen as products of decayed civilizations. It was thus that China and Persia, Burma and Egypt, Turkey and Ethiopia were presented. Only Japan escaped this conceptual trap, and then because it Westernized so rapidly. Thus, the modern Europeans were akin to the Classical Greeks resisting Persia under Xerxes and Darius, while their generals were latter-day Alexanders the Great. The notion of Western warfare therefore drew on strong cultural impulses and these gave it an identity that helped explain and justify success. Christian providentialization and cultural superiority were also present in the explanation of technological progress, which, in turn, was held to demonstrate them. Different commentators presented this account with contrasting emphases, but it was, nevertheless, a key element in the positioning and explanation of warfare.

The Western interpretation of warfare in terms of Christian providentialism and Western cultural superiority became far less prominent in the twentieth century, although it was definitely to the fore in the opening stages of the First World War. After that, there was a shift away from nineteenth-century notions, although again for varied reasons that were of different importance for particular commentators. First, the emphasis from 1914 to 1989 on struggle or confrontation within the Western world – the assassinations that launched the First World War at Sarajevo, to the Fall of the Berlin Wall that ended the Cold War – did not encourage such a clear-cut and consistent cultural and moral approach as the 'less developed' world was not so consistently the sphere of imperial warfare. Looked at differently, however, such approaches were deployed during both the two World Wars and the Cold War, but they were short-term and particularly associated with one or other side. Thus, German assumptions of a right to rule and of cultural superiority were discredited with the failure to establish a German empire in Europe, while Communist counterparts also proved unsuccessful.

Second, the failure of the West in sustaining imperial rule or even post-imperial power across the Third World was a prominent feature of the period 1919–75, and, more particularly, 1945–75. Ideologies of cultural superiority did not provide victory for the French in Indo-China and could not ensure lasting domestic support for the Portuguese government in its resistance to insurgencies in their African colonies in 1961–74.

Lastly, the warfare of the age of total war appeared so different to what had come before that historicist accounts of conflict seemed redundant. The Western Way of War was not thus to the fore in the late twentieth century. Indeed, one of the key concepts of the 1990s, the Revolution in Military Affairs (RMA) was particularly unreceptive to such a designation, because its technological impetus and definition were presented as possibly for diffusion across cultural boundaries.

The 2000s, however, witnessed a rediscovery of the concept of the Western Way of War, most prominently with the writings of the American historian Victor Davis Hanson, although not only with him. This rediscovery was very presentist in character, resting as it did on the concatenation of expeditionary warfare and the 'War on Terror' with the need to provide a new doctrine and exegesis to replace, or at least supplement, the RMA. Hanson, an expert on warfare in Classical Greece, sought to provide reassurance and certainty, arguing that Western cultural factors brought strength and success, and that, once this was understood, it should encourage a firmness of purpose. He also proposed a clear lineage, linking the ancient world to modern conflict.

The details of Hanson's approach have been much criticized and its lacunae and flaws are clearly highlighted, not least with the absence of the clear linkage he proposed between the citizens' army of ancient Athens and such armies in the West over the last quarter millennium; but less attention has been devoted to a more central flaw, that of essentialism or a central identity. In short, whatever the questionable nature of the belief in a Western Way of War having certain characteristics, there is the issue of whether there is something that can be defined as a Western Way of War.

The questioning of the latter can come from a number of directions. It can be argued that the key element is that of national military culture and that there was/is such a powerful variety among the latter that the idea of an aggregate Western Way of War falls to the side. It can also be suggested that the national dimension has been overplayed, an argument that can be made not in order to privilege a Western Way of War, but, instead, because most military development is task-driven, and changes in the context that condition and affect tasks are crucial. For example, talk of a distinctive and consistent Way of War means little for militaries and societies that have to adapt to the changes entailed by switching into and out of the practice and consequences of conscription, or between conventional and counter-insurgency conflict.

Variety occurs across space as well as time. A Western Way of War in 1650 would have had to encompass the 'regular' forces of Western Europe, the greater role for cavalry in Eastern Europe, as well as colonial forces, most obviously in Latin America, and those thrown forward by civil wars. Moreover, it would be necessary to show that these forces were recognizably different in type from those seen elsewhere in Eurasia. Once external contrasts are taken out of consideration, were the force structures and doctrines sufficiently contrasting to non-European/Western counterparts to think in terms of distinctive European patterns, whether or not they were to be aggregated in terms of a Western Way of War? The answer is probably not. In particular, there was considerable overlap between methods of warmaking and fighting in Eastern Europe across the Christian–Muslim divide. Comparisons with the Ottoman Empire (Turkey) can then be extrapolated by asking about the extent of the contrast between, say, the armies of Tsar Alexis of Russia and John Sobieski of Poland or those of the Kangzi Emperor in China and Aurangzeb, his Mughal counterpart in India.

If contrasts between Western and non-Western warfare emerge more clearly by 1750 and, even more, 1850, it can be asked whether this was due to essential differences or to stages in a developmental process, the latter a thesis advanced by those interested in Westernization and diffusion, and, notably, in some of the writing on Indian military history; or to contingency. Moreover, contrasts between West and non-West have to be set alongside a reality of variety in both West and non-West, with these variations also involving overlap with the other category. This situation has remained the case throughout the nineteenth and twentieth centuries and into the present age.

Parallels are also instructive. The ability of governments, not limited to Western ones, to impose their will on the state or nation in order ultimately to achieve their objectives, and the extent to which they are willing to expend resources, including population, to achieve that end, are crucial. If this warmaking is defined as a 'Western' characteristic, then, however, as a key qualification, it has to be noted that war among states beyond the West, such as between the Ottoman and Persian Empires, or the recent Iran–Iraq and India–Pakistan Wars, were conducted in an analogous fashion. Indeed, the ability and willingness of these governments to sustain heavy casualties to achieve their objectives suggests that the notion of a distinctive Western way of war should be questioned or perhaps simply stated as the way governments wage war, irrespective of geographic region.

If the idea of a distinctive Western Way of War is therefore suspect from a number of different directions, this does not mean that a Western-dominated mindset has not conditioned much of our (Western) understanding of warfare, with war understood in terms of a largely Western vision. A similar point can be made elsewhere, and the related deficiencies could also be serious. For example, the Chinese understanding of war in the nineteenth century was even more flawed than its Western counterpart because the relevant range of experience was more limited (no recent transoceanic or naval warfare), and the same point can be made about other states and 'cultures', whatever the latter are to be understood as meaning.

Whether belief in a Western Way of War can be successfully detached from a Western-dominated mindset is unclear, but the freedom of expression in the West and the breadth of scholarly discussion (within the academy but also outside it) offer some encouragement on this head. The extent of sophisticated debate within the American military and related military academies and think-tanks is particularly impressive. In large part, there has been a strong critique not only of the RMA but also of any notion of technological determinism.

There has also been much call for a need for task-based warfare rather than the capability-centred emphasis on output: force delivered, for example bombs dropped. An interest in outcome certainly entails an attempt to place warfare more centrally in its political context. All this can be seen as conforming to or clashing with the/a Western Way of War, which simply highlights the questionable nature of the latter concept if it is to be employed as a coherent analytical tool and building block.

Yet, approached differently, it is precisely because the idea of a Western Way of War is so loose that it has proved so valuable, especially to broad-brush writers. Indeed, it is the very looseness of concepts that makes them useful. It can be argued that this feature is particularly the case with military history, not least because many of the writers are popular historians or military figures who are not adept at, or interested in, sophisticated (or any) conceptual discussions. The latter point suggests that the Western Way of War still has considerable mileage. Like many ideas it fills a gap. As such, it offers a parallel to such concepts as the early-modern European Military Revolution (see pp. 61–76). The extension of the idea of military revolution indicates the value attached to any concept that is available.

This situation again, in part, is a reflection of the degree to which the field often lacks intellectual sophistication, although, looked at differently, the treatment of military developments by specialists in more conceptual fields, such as sociology and politics, is scarcely encouraging. Moreover, it would be inaccurate to suggest that military affairs lack a changing vocabulary. The large-scale diffusion from the 1980s of the concept of the operational dimension of conflict is particularly instructive, as is a more general engagement with doctrine. Furthermore, in the 2000s, the range of discussion of COIN (Counter-Insurgency) doctrine and methods repays attention as evidence of a capacity for a considered response to circumstances and experience.

Whether other societies have different response methods and models is unclear, for one of the problems that is worth considering is the extent to which there is a lack of published critical discussion of the situation by many other societies. Indeed, however much Western-centric perspectives are to be criticized, they are less flawed than what appears to be on offer elsewhere. For example, it is unclear how much the insurgents in Iraq or the Taliban have a sense of the wider parameters of military change. Looked at differently, they locate their own activities in an experience that provides not only motivation but also an ability to respond to challenges. This situation was seen in Afghanistan with the response, first, to the Red Army in the 1980s and, second, to Western military power in the 2000s.

Yet, considered in another light, the Iraqi insurgents, like the Taliban, found that their ideas and practices brought less success than they had anticipated, and this failure contributed to a general inability of warmaking in 2001–8 to achieve desired results. The extent to which this inability reflected widespread conceptual limitations, both in the West and in the non-West (in so far as they can be aggregated and distinguished), repays attention. It also suggests that criticism of simple practices of Western-centred analysis should be set in a wider context of failure, and, more generally, underlines the need for comparative assessment when judging capability. That is not simply the case for historians, but also for those considering war today as well as its likely future development.

Selected Further Reading

GENERAL

Black, J. *Rethinking Military History* (2004).

Black, J. *Introduction to Global Military History* (2005).

Linn, B. M. *The Echo of Battle. The Army's Way of War* (2007).

Lorge, P. *The Asian Military Revolution. From Gunpowder to the Bomb* (2008).

Lynn, J. A. *Battle. A History of Combat and Culture. From Ancient Greece to Modern America* (2003).

Morillo, S., Black, J. and Lococo, P., *War in World History* (2009).

Stone, D. R. *A Military History of Russia. From Ivan the Terrible to the War in Chechnya* (2006).

CHAPTER 1

Carman, J. and A. Harding (eds), *Ancient Warfare* (1999).

Doyne, D. *The First Armies* (2001).

Graff, D. *Medieval Chinese Warfare, 300–900* (2001).

Hamblin, W. J. *Warfare in the Ancient Near East to 1600 BC* (2006).

Hanson, V. D. *The Western Way of War: Infantry Battle in Classical Greece* (1989).

Keeley, L. H. *War before Civilisation: The Myth of the Peaceful Savage* (1996).

Otterbein, K. *How War Began* (2004).

Partridge, R. *Fighting Pharaohs: Weapons and Warfare in Ancient Egypt* (2002).

Saggs, H. W. F. *The Might that Was Assyria* (1994).

Sidebotham, H. *Ancient Warfare: A Very Short Introduction* (2004).

Van Wees, H. *Greek Warfare: Myths and Realities* (2004).

CHAPTER 2

France, J. *Western Warfare in the Age of the Crusades, 1000–1300* (1999).

Haldon, J. *Warfare, State and Society in the Byzantine World, 560–1204* (1999).

Kennedy, H. *The Armies of the Caliphs. Military and Society in the Early Islamic State* (2001).

Rose, S. *Medieval Naval Warfare, 1000–1500* (2001).

Tyerman, C. *God's War: A New History of the Crusades* (2006).

CHAPTER 3

Black, J. M. *European Warfare, 1494–1660* (2002).

Capponi, N. *Victory of the West: The Story of the Battle of Lepanto* (2006).

Chase, K. *Firearms. A Global History to 1700* (2003).

Davies, B. L. *Warfare, State and Society on the Black Sea Steppe, 1500–1700* (2007).

Fissel, M. C. *English Warfare, 1511–1642* (2001).

Glete, J. *War and the State in Early Modern Europe* (2001).

Gommans, J. *Mughal Warfare* (2002).

Murphey, R. *Ottoman Warfare* (2000).

Parker, G. *The Military Revolution: Military Innovation and the Rise of the West, 1500–1800* (2 edn 1996).

Steele, B. D. and T. Dorland (eds), *The Heirs of Archimedes. Science and the Art of War through the Age of Enlightenment* (2005).

Thornton, J. K. *Warfare in Atlantic Africa, 1500–1800* (1999).

CHAPTER 4

Black, J. *European Warfare in a Global Context, 1660–1815* (2007).

Harding, R. *Seapower and Naval Warfare, 1650–1830* (1999).

Higginbotham, D. (ed.), *George Washington Reconsidered* (2001).

Rodger, N. A. M. *The Command of the Ocean. A Naval History of Britain, 1649–1815* (2004).

Starkey, A. *European and Native American Warfare, 1675–1815* (1998).

Starkey, A. *War in the Age of Enlightenment, 1700–1789* (2003).

Ward, H. M. *The War of Independence and the Transformation of American Society* (1999).

Wilson, P. *German Armies. War and German Society, 1648–1806* (1998).

CHAPTER 5

Black, J. *The Age of Total War, 1860–1945* (2006).

Black, J. *Nineteenth-Century Warfare* (2009).

Buckley, J. *Air Power in the Age of Total War* (1998).

Connelly, O. *The Wars of the French Revolution and Napoleon* (2006).

Cooper, R. G. S. *The Anglo-Maratha Campaigns and the Contest for India* (2003).

Elleman, B. A. *Modern Chinese Warfare, 1795–1989* (2001).

Esdaile, C. *Napoleon's Wars* (2007).

Ferguson, N. *The War of the World* (2006).

Heuser, B. *Reading Clausewitz* (2000).

Howard, M. *The First World War* (2002).

Sondhaus, L. *Naval Warfare, 1815–1914* (2000).

Sondhaus, L. *Navies in Modern World History* (2004).

Vandervort, B. *Wars of Imperial Conquest in Africa, 1830–1914* (1998).

Vandervort, B. *Indian Wars of Canada, Mexico and the United States, 1812–1900* (2005).

CHAPTER 6

Beckett, I. F. *Modern Insurgencies and Counter-Insurgencies* (2001).

Black, J. *War since 1945* (2004).

Black, J. *War since 1990* (2009).

Bregman, A. *Israel's Wars, 1947–1993* (2000).

Clayton, A. *Frontiersmen: Warfare in Africa Since 1950* (1998).

Lewis, A. R. *The American Culture of War* (2007).

Murray W. and R. H. Scales, *The Iraq War* (2003).

Tucker, S. *Vietnam* (1999).

Index